Watercolors by Kandinsky

AT THE GUGGENHEIM MUSEUM

A selection from the Solomon R. Guggenheim Museum and the Hilla von Rebay Foundation

Introductory essay by Susan B. Hirschfeld

GUGGENHEIM MUSEUM

New York

©The Solomon R. Guggenheim Foundation, New York, 1991
All rights reserved
ISBN: 0–89207–069–2 (hardcover)
ISBN: 0–89207–070–6 (softcover)
Printed in Spain

Published by the Guggenheim Museum
1071 Fifth Avenue, New York, New York 10128

Distributed by Rizzoli International Publications, Inc.
300 Park Avenue South, New York, New York 10010

Design by Cara Galowitz and Juan Ariño
Color separations and printing by El Viso, Madrid
Color photography by David Heald

Cover: *Bogen und Spitze* (*Arc and Point*), February 1923
Watercolor, India ink, and pencil on paper
46.5 x 42 cm (18 $^5/_{16}$ x 16 $^9/_{16}$ inches)
Solomon R. Guggenheim Museum

PREFACE

Thomas Krens

From its inception more than a half century ago, the collection at the heart of the Guggenheim Museum has been assembled based on a strategy that favors depth over breadth. In no area is this truer than in the holdings of works by Vasily Kandinsky, for which the Guggenheim's founding director, Hilla Rebay, had a passion. Her deeply felt affinity with Kandinsky's ideas about art coincided with her vision of a museum devoted to non-objective painting. This museum came to fruition as a result of Rebay's close collaboration with Solomon R. Guggenheim. Although the Guggenheim Museum is no longer bound to a strict ideology that rejects figurative art, it still maintains its strong commitment to artists whose work pushes—and in doing so redefines—the boundaries of modern art.

The museum has become a prime resource for all those interested in Kandinsky's work, and its commitment to research on it is ongoing. But Solomon Guggenheim's intentions would not be best served without attempting to make his gift more widely accessible. This book and the exhibition that suggested it arose from a continuing effort to find new ways to present the Guggenheim's treasures to the public.

The Guggenheim is an amalgam of many collections that maintain their identities within the context of the museum. This is true of our Kandinsky holdings as well. But no matter how we categorize Kandinsky's works of art—as part of Solomon R. Guggenheim's bequest; the Hilla Rebay Collection, incorporated into the Guggenheim Museum in 1971; or the Hilla von Rebay Foundation collection, which has been housed at the Guggenheim since 1970—his vision is an enduring one. Kandinsky's legacy is one that we are proud to steward, and even prouder to share.

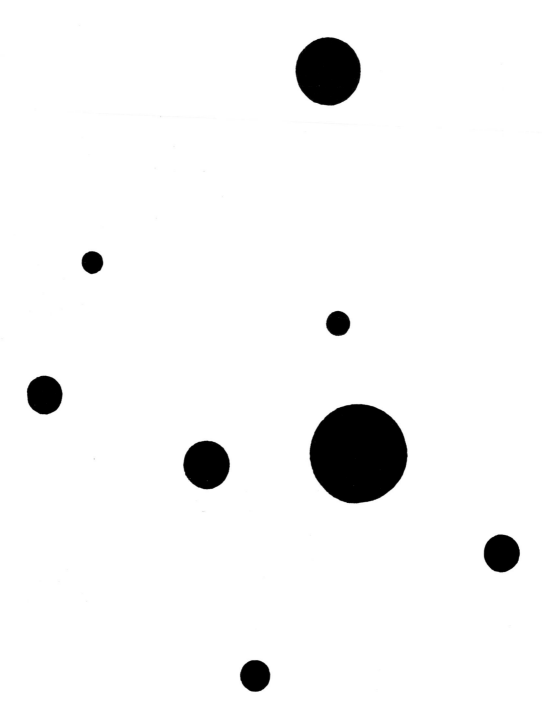

Diagram 3
Point
9 points in ascent (emphasis upon the diagonal d-a through weight)

WATERCOLORS BY KANDINSKY

Susan B. Hirschfeld

Two of the most important collections of works by Vasily Kandinsky—those belonging to the Solomon R. Guggenheim Foundation and the Hilla von Rebay Foundation—originated with Hilla Rebay, a German artist whose passionate advocacy of non-objective painting greatly influenced the formation and evolution of the Guggenheim Museum. It was she who introduced Solomon Guggenheim to the avant-garde painters of the 1920s and 1930s who would come to be recognized as pioneers of modern art. According to Rebay, there was no higher art than non-objective painting, which, in her mind, differed greatly from abstraction. Rebay believed that abstract art was derived from nature, while the the pure "non-objective picture stands by itself as an entirely free creation, conceived out of the intuitive enjoyment of space. It is the visual essence of rhythmic balance in form, design and color."[1] Many of Rebay's ideas about non-objective art and its power to change society were inspired by Vasily Kandinsky, whom she admired above all other artists. And, perhaps more than any other twentieth-century painter, Kandinsky has been closely linked to the history of the Solomon R. Guggenheim Museum.

Rebay immigrated to New York in January 1927 at the age of thirty-six.[2] That fall she became acquainted with Solomon Guggenheim and his wife, Irene Rothschild, and was soon acting as art adviser to the prosperous businessman. In the summer of 1929, Rebay introduced Guggenheim to Kandinsky at his studio at the Dessau Bauhaus, and Guggenheim purchased a major oil, *Composition 8*. This was the start of a period of continuous acquisitions of Kandinsky's watercolors and oils. During the next seven years, Rebay and Guggenheim made subsequent trips to Europe and met other major avant-garde painters, often purchasing works directly from them. At the same time, Rebay began to form her own collection by purchase, by exchanging works that she had painted for those of other artists, and through gifts from, among others, Robert Delaunay, Albert Gleizes, László Moholy-Nagy, and Guggenheim.[3] Within a decade, Guggenheim had amassed a major collection that could be shared with the public. In 1937 he transferred canvases by Rudolf Bauer, Marc Chagall, Delaunay, Lyonel Feininger, Gleizes, Paul Klee, Fernand Léger, and Kandinsky to a foundation he established in New York City that was empowered to operate a museum.

1. Forty-year-old Vasily Kandinsky, depicted in a 1906 color woodcut made by his companion, the artist Gabriele Münter.
Solomon R. Guggenheim Museum

2. facing page:
Diagram and caption from the Museum of Non-Objective Painting's English edition of *Point and Line to Plane*, published in 1947.

The original gift of 145 paintings included twenty-seven oils and six watercolors by Kandinsky. The Solomon R. Guggenheim Museum of Non-Objective Painting opened in rented galleries at 24 East 54th Street on May 31, 1939, and Rebay was named its first director.[4] Guggenheim made additional gifts to the collection in 1940 and 1941; with the latter came twenty-one works by Kandinsky. When Guggenheim died in November 1949, the remaining paintings in his private collection, including two more Kandinskys, were bequeathed to the foundation. This final gift brought the total Kandinsky holdings of the foundation to more than 180 works. Since that time the collection has been refined through both sales and acquisitions, particularly in the area of prints. Together with the important works held by the Hilla von Rebay Foundation, which have been on deposit at the museum since 1970, the Guggenheim collection encompasses more than 205 objects by Kandinsky, including oils, watercolors, drawings, and prints, as well as valuable documentary and archival materials. Along with the State museums of the Soviet Union, the Gabriele Münter Collection at the Städtische Galerie im Lenbachhaus in Munich, and the collection that Nina Kandinsky bequeathed to the Musée national d'art moderne in Paris, the Guggenheim Museum is one of the world's prime repositories of Kandinsky's artistic legacy.

The watercolors that Kandinsky executed throughout most of his career are an important part of the collection, and of Kandinsky's oeuvre itself. Those at the Guggenheim range in date from about 1911, when the artist was living in Munich and had already established himself as a major avant-gardist with an international reputation, to 1941, just three years prior to his death in Neuilly-sur-Seine. The watercolors demonstrate a remarkable technical expertise with the liquid pigment, and, like the artist's oil and tempera paintings, an extraordinary degree of experimentation. Often executed with other media such as pencil, ink, gouache, bronze-powder paint, and opaque white, Kandinsky's watercolors range from freely brushed compositions of pure, clear color to those produced with stencils and layers of finely spattered paint.

Unlike most other painting materials, watercolor is transparent rather than opaque, more like a stain than a continuous film or layer of pigment. Paintings with watercolor rely on the white of the paper for their whites and paler tints while the grain of the sheet contributes to the final effect of the picture. Indeed, the different ways that color is taken from the brush by the high and low areas of the grain, as well as the degree of saturation, create varied surface textures that contribute a depth and range of tone that is peculiar to this medium. The fluid, runny quality of watercolor pigments, as well as their essential transparent quality, demand a considerable degree of technical skill. Close examination of Kandinsky's watercolors reveals virtually no errors or reworkings and that, for the most part, the artist painted his watercolors on high-quality paper.[5]

Whether as independent works of art or as studies for oil paintings, the watercolors chart the evolution of Kandinsky's oeuvre. It is therefore possible to trace the development of the artist's innovative abstract idiom by focusing on a broad selection of works in this medium, while demonstrating the richness and depth of the Guggenheim Museum's extensive holdings.

Vasily Vasilievich Kandinsky was born in Moscow on December 4, 1866, to Vasily, a tea merchant, and Lidia Tikheeva.[6] In 1871 the family moved to Odessa, where the young Kandinsky attended the Gymnasium and learned to play the cello and piano. He studied law and economics at the University of Moscow in 1886 and in 1889 journeyed to the Vologda province in northern Russia on an anthropological expedition. According to his "Reminiscences," an autobiographical account of his early years published in 1913, the folk art Kandinsky encountered on this trip, in particular the intensely colored, vigorously designed decorations inside the peasants' homes, deeply impressed him.[7]

The "Reminiscences" are filled with enthusiastic accounts of other early influences. He was profoundly moved by the effects of color disengaged from subject matter when he saw one of Claude Monet's Haystack paintings at a Moscow exhibition and failed to recognize the image. From this experience he would come to realize that the necessity of "objects . . . as an essential element within the picture" had been "discredited."[8] Kandinsky considered his discovery in 1889 of the values of light and color in Rembrandt's paintings among his most important early experiences. In his "Reminiscences," the artist also recalled how a performance of Wagner's *Lohengrin* led to his awakening knowledge of the relationship between music and painting:

> *Lohengrin*, on the other hand, seemed to me the complete realization of that Moscow. The violins, the deep tones of the basses, and especially the wind instruments at that time embodied for me all the power of that pre-nocturnal hour. I saw all my colors in my mind; they stood before my eyes. Wild, almost crazy lines were sketched in front of me. I did not dare use the expression that Wagner had painted "my hour" musically. It became, however, quite clear to me that . . . painting could develop just such powers as music possesses.[9]

From this time, Kandinsky was fascinated with music's ability to convey emotions without the help of representation and he longed to provide painting with the same independence from nature that gave music its universal power. Later in his career he would seek to achieve the effects of musical sonority in his work through discords, harmonies, and rhythms produced by the juxtaposition of colors, shapes, and lines.

In 1892 Kandinsky concluded his university studies and passed his examinations in law. The following year he began to teach law at the University of Moscow, but, as he explained in his "Reminiscences," despite his love for the law his encounters with art were more deeply felt.[10] In 1895 he became the artistic director of a printing firm in Moscow, where he became acquainted with various graphic techniques.[11] One year later, Kandinsky declined an offer to teach law at the University of Dorpat. Instead, he would move to Munich to devote himself to the study of painting.

The capital of Bavaria and one of Europe's leading cultural centers, Munich had attracted many other Russians, including the artists Vladimir von Bechtejeff, David Burliuk, Igor Grabar, Alexej Jawlensky, Dmitrii Kardovsky, and Marianne von Werefkin, and the dancer Alexander Sacharoff. Soon after his arrival, Kandinsky enrolled in the painting school of the Yugoslav Anton Ažbe, where he met Jawlensky and von Werefkin. Ažbe, a gifted artist who was known for his use of pure colors applied directly to the canvas, taught drawing from the nude and anatomy. The

3. Watercolor sketches depicting female nudes and St. Hubertus, dating from Kandinsky's years as a pupil in Anton Ažbe's Munich studio. (8 ¼ x 12 ⁷/₁₆ inches.) Städtische Galerie im Lenbachhaus, Munich (GMS 441)

Lenbachhaus in Munich possesses small ink-and-watercolor studies by Kandinsky, depicting male and female nudes, that date from this period (fig. 3). Although Ažbe emphasized the importance of anatomy, Kandinsky's works display less interest in observing nature than in exploring the possibilities of line and contrasts of light and dark. Kandinsky remained in Ažbe's studio for two years, but found both the academic courses and the crowded conditions stifling and preferred to spend time painting on his own, often outdoors.[12]

In 1900 Kandinsky was accepted into the atelier of Franz von Stuck at the Munich Academy. Stuck was known for his exceptional skill as a draftsman and for his defiance of the established Munich School of historical painting. He was regarded as an excellent, exciting instructor; the combination of artistic freedom he allowed his students and his iconoclastic style of painting were, no doubt, particularly attractive to Kandinsky. The sensuous and symbolic content of Stuck's work typified a new, expressive style that was prevalent in Munich at the turn of the century. Jugendstil, the German counterpart of Art Nouveau, took its name from *Jugend* (*Youth*), a contemporary literary and artistic periodical that expressed a left-liberal political viewpoint. Deriving its forms from nature rather than from the man-made world, Jugendstil was basically ornamental. It was characterized by rhythmic, sinuous lines, organic shapes, and broad, flat areas of pure and striking color. Jugendstil was embraced by a number of young artists, who applied its principles to sculpture, architecture, design, and crafts. The Munich Secession, a progressive artists' association that had been formed in 1892 by artists who sought to bring more selective and international exhibitions to the city, presented works by Jugendstil artists as early as 1897. It is probable that Kandinsky visited these exhibitions, which received substantial coverage in the press.[13]

Hoping to provide even greater opportunities for younger artists who were not acceptable to the Secession, Kandinsky and a diverse group of painters, sculptors, and writers founded the Phalanx exhibition society in May 1901 in order to stage exhibitions that would stimulate Munich's artistic climate. Kandinsky designed the poster for the first Phalanx exhibition, which took place in August (fig. 4).[14] The mosaic-like border, flat forms, and flowing linearity of the letters at the top and bottom create an emphatically decorative work. Its design was inspired by an earlier example by Stuck and reflects the style of Jugendstil illustration of the period. Despite Kandinsky's apparent lack of formal training with the techniques of printmaking, the poster, among the first known graphic works by the artist, demonstrates an extraordinary understanding of the graphic medium and its particular capabilities for rendering line, form, and tonal effects.

From 1902 to 1904 Kandinsky produced more than forty woodcuts using the Japanese method of printing.[15] In the woodcuts (see, for example, fig. 5), the importance of sinuous, curvilinear patterns and areas of dark and light that contrast with bold patches of color reveal Kandinsky's interest in the decorative elements of Jugendstil design, while the rather melancholy mood and romantic subject matter refer back to more traditional sources. During his early years in Munich, Kandinsky often depicted romantic, fairy-tale subjects, landscapes, knights, and horseback riders as well as nostalgic images of his Russian homeland.

Kandinsky experimented with a variety of media at this time; he painted with oils and tempera, ground his own pigments, and often combined these with other substances such as glues, plaster, clay, and ground eggshells. Between 1901 and 1908 he

4. The influence of Franz von Stuck, his second Munich teacher, is strongly felt in the 1901 poster Kandinsky designed for the first Phalanx exhibition. (Color lithograph; image: 18 x 23 1/4 inches.)
Solomon R. Guggenheim Museum
Gift, Kenneth C. Lindsay, 1963

5. *Singer*, a 1903 color woodcut in which Kandinsky blended the styles of French and Russian Symbolism with Art Nouveau. (Image: 7 7/8 x 5 3/4 inches.)
Solomon R. Guggenheim Museum

6. Painted in 1905, *Tunisian Sheep Festival*
belongs to the *farbige Zeichnungen*.
(Tempera on board with colored paper,
16 ¹/₂ x 22 ¹/₂ inches.)
Solomon R. Guggenheim Museum

7. *Riding Couple* (1907), like other
paintings of the period, is more
naturalistic than contemporary
woodcuts; the images are derived from
Russian fairy tales. (Oil on canvas,
21 ¹¹/₁₆ x 19 ⁷/₈ inches.)
Städtische Galerie im Lenbachhaus, Munich
(GMS 26)

executed a dramatic group of temperas he called *"farbige Zeichnungen"* or "colored drawings." Kandinsky's contemporary oils reflect his concern with Impressionist technique and naturalistic effect, whereas the *farbige Zeichnungen* are clearly more experimental. In *Fête de moutons (Tunisian Sheep Festival*, 1905, fig. 6), for example, the mood and method of execution are quite different. Here, an exotic, busy marketplace emerges from the indeterminate space of the dark paper support.[16] Distinct, flat areas and shapes of pigment define figures, bringing the fanciful picture to life. Like the early woodcuts, the colored drawings present clearly articulated images against dark, ambiguous backgrounds. Foregrounds and backgrounds are often merged into a single dark surface and both colored and dark areas take on qualities of autonomous, abstract forms. Kandinsky was careful to distinguish the *farbige Zeichnungen* from his oils, watercolors, and prints and kept a separate handlist of the paintings made with tempera.[17] Nevertheless, the stylistic affinities between the early woodcuts and the colored drawings, as well as their reliance on Russian and French Symbolism, underscore the close relationship between these contemporaneous groups of works.

In the winter of 1901–02 members of the Phalanx society founded a school where students took classes in still life and studied sketching and modeling. Kandinsky taught painting and drawing from the nude. One of his students was Gabriele Münter, a young German artist who enrolled in 1902. A close relationship developed between them, and they remained companions until the outbreak of World War I. Between 1903 and 1909 Kandinsky traveled a great deal, with Münter often accompanying him. In 1903 he returned to Russia and briefly visited Odessa and Moscow, passing through Venice and Vienna, and by the end of 1904 he had gone to the Netherlands and Paris. In May 1906 the couple sojourned in Paris for about a month before moving to Sèvres, just outside the city, where they lived for a year.

During this period Kandinsky became involved with French art and the Paris art world. He exhibited at the Salon d'Automne in Paris from 1905 to 1910 and showed with the Post-Impressionists, Nabis, and Fauves at the Salon des Indépendants in 1907. He would have seen paintings by Gauguin, van Gogh, and Matisse and his fellow Fauves. Their dramatic and expressive use of pure, vivid color would have an impact on Kandinsky as the hues in his own oils gradually became more brilliant and evocative. *Reitendes Paar (Riding Couple*, fig. 7) of ca. 1907, one of the most beautiful of the artist's many nostalgic scenes of Russia from this period, was painted during Kandinsky's stay in Paris. In the oil the viewer is struck by the colorful, jewel-like pattern of dots that cover the entire surface of the canvas. The dots and flecks of blues, greens, oranges, yellows, pinks, and reds lend the work vitality; despite the relatively naturalistic approach, the mosaic pattern formed by the colored dots creates a rich, embroidered effect that removes the scene from the realm of everyday life.

The summer of 1908 marked Kandinsky's and Münter's first trip to Murnau, a small village south of Munich near the Bavarian Alps. Often joined by Jawlensky and von Werefkin, Kandinsky and Münter split their time between Murnau and Munich from 1909 until the outbreak of World War I. Kandinsky loved the Bavarian folk art he saw everywhere in Murnau. He and his colleagues began to experiment with these crafts, producing *Hinterglasmalereien* (paintings on glass), wood carvings, reliefs, and decorated furniture. Especially important to Kandinsky was the expressive potential of the naive techniques and glowing colors of the peasants' religious art, which he felt directly and forcefully conveyed universal spiritual messages.

While in the countryside, Kandinsky and his friends began to bring their easels outdoors to capture scenes of the surrounding landscape. By the summer of 1908 Kandinsky was already painting the towers, rolling hills, and village houses of Murnau in canvases dominated by striking arrangements of vivid patches and lines of reds,

8. The bold colors and experimental brushwork of *Blue Mountain* (1908–09) signal the emergence of the artist's personal painting style. (Oil on canvas, 41 ¼ x 38 inches.)
Solomon R. Guggenheim Museum
Gift, Solomon R. Guggenheim, 1941

greens, violets, and yellows. *Der blaue Berg (Blue Mountain*, fig. 8), a major oil of 1908–09, reveals a further stage in Kandinsky's transition toward abstraction. Recognizable imagery, while still apparent, has become less important in relation to abstract color forms. The patterns of blue, red, and yellow dabs of pigment, as well as the gestural brushwork, underscore the rhythms suggested by the horses and riders galloping across the canvas. The bounding of broad areas of bright, radiant color by dark black lines brings to mind compositions in stained-glass windows and *Hinterglasmalereien*. This work shows how Kandinsky had assimilated both the intense Fauvist color and the traditional techniques of local Bavarian artisans to produce a unique, personal style.

In 1909 Kandinsky, Jawlensky, and others, dissatisfied with exhibition opportunities available in Munich for vanguard artists, formed the NKVM (Neue Künstlervereinigung München, or New Artists' Association Munich). Kandinsky was elected president of the NKVM, which was larger and more international than Phalanx, and participated in the society's first two exhibitions, at the Moderne Galerie Thannhauser in Munich. He also made original designs for the society's poster and letterhead.

Kandinsky completed the manuscript for *Über das Geistige in der Kunst (On the Spiritual in Art)* in 1910. In this major treatise he discussed the spiritual basis of art and the need for painting that was capable of expressing inner life with forms derived from the external world. What the observer seeks in the work of art, he noted, is "either the pure imitation of nature, serving practical ends (such as portraiture . . .), or an imitation of nature that comprises a specific interpretation ('Impressionist' painting), or, ultimately, a particular state of mind clothed in the forms of nature (which one calls 'mood'). All these forms, if truly artistic, fulfill their purpose and provide . . . spiritual nourishment—but particularly in the third example, where the spectator finds a sympathetic vibration within his own soul. Moreover, a sympathetic—or even an unsympathetic—vibration cannot remain merely empty or superficial; on the contrary, the 'mood' of the work can intensify—and transform—the mood of the spectator. In any case, such works prevent the soul from becoming coarsened."[18]

On the Spiritual in Art helped disseminate and foster acceptance of Kandinsky's ideas, including those on the relationship between painting and music. In the book, he describes the difficult task of the painter, "who sees that the imitation of natural appearances, however artistic, is not for him—the kind of creative artist who wants, and has to, express his own inner world—sees with envy how naturally and easily such goals can be attained in music, the least material of the arts today. Understandably, he may turn toward it and try to find the same means in his own art. Hence the current search for rhythm in painting, for mathematical, abstract construction, the value placed today upon the repetition of color-tones, the way colors are set in motion."[19]

Kandinsky firmly believed in the ability of a language of basic forms and colors to express abstract ideas or feelings. According to him, different combinations of colors and shapes convey "different spiritual values," although certain colors and shapes are interrelated: "Sharp colors have a stronger sound in sharp forms (e.g., yellow in a triangle). The effect of deeper colors is emphasized by rounded forms (e.g., blue in a circle)."[20] Much of Kandinsky's subsequent pedagogical writings, his teaching, and the geometric style of his later works of the 1920s and 1930s are predicated on these early theories. In *On the Spiritual in Art* Kandinsky cited other influences on his work, including the writing of Maurice Maeterlinck, the music of Mussorgsky, Schönberg, Aleksandr Scriabin, and Wagner, and the art of Cézanne, Matisse, and Picasso. He also mentioned the Theosophical Society and the occult writings of Madame Blavatsky as having influenced his thinking about abstraction.[21]

During the period that Kandinsky was writing *On the Spiritual in Art*, he met Franz Marc and August Macke in connection with the NKVM exhibition held at the Moderne Galerie in 1910. Due to increasing conflicts between Kandinsky's avant-garde circle and the more conservative membership of the NKVM, Kandinsky resigned his position as president in 1911. In December, Kandinsky, Marc, Münter, and fellow artist Alfred Kubin withdrew from the NKVM after the jury for the third exhibition rejected Kandinsky's *Composition V* (1911, Private Collection, Switzerland). By this time Kandinsky and Marc had already begun to plan the *Almanach der Blaue Reiter* (*Blue Rider Almanac*). In a letter of June 19, 1911, Kandinsky presented his ideas for the almanac to Marc:

> A kind of almanac (yearbook) with reproductions and articles . . . and a *chronicle*!! that is, reports on exhibitions reviewed by artists, and artists alone. In the book the entire year must be reflected; and a link to the past as well as a ray to the future must give this mirror its full life. . . . We will put an Egyptian work beside a small Zeh [the last name of two talented children], a Chinese work beside a Rousseau, a folk print beside a Picasso, and the like! Eventually we will attract poets and musicians.[22]

The pace of work on the almanac accelerated when the two artists broke with the NKVM and within weeks mounted the first Blaue Reiter exhibition. A second exhibition opened at the Galerie Hans Goltz in Munich in February 1912.

Kandinsky's ideas were realized that spring when the *Blue Rider Almanac* was published. The volume contained articles by editors Kandinsky and Marc, David Burliuk, Macke, the composers Schönberg and Thomas de Hartmann, and others. More than 140 works, ranging from primitive art objects and Bavarian folk art to paintings by Kandinsky, Marc, Cézanne, Robert Delaunay, Henri Le Fauconnier, El Greco, Matisse, Henri Rousseau, and Vincent van Gogh were reproduced. Musical scores by Alban Berg, Schönberg, and Anton von Webern were also published. Kandinsky's contributions included an essay, "Über Bühnenkomposition" ("On Stage Composition"), and the script for *Der gelbe Klang* (*The Yellow Sound*), an abstract stage composition that he had begun to write in the spring of 1909.

When he received the finished almanac, Marc wrote to Kandinsky:

> Now that I am confronted with the *fait accompli*, I am getting used to it,
> at least I have to. The impression of the book is after all fabulous. I was
> so happy to see it before me finally finished. I am sure of one thing: many
> silent admirers in the land and many young forces will thank us secretly,
> they will be enchanted with the book and will judge the world by it.[23]

Due to the success of the first edition, a second printing was published in 1914. A second volume was planned, but, because of the war, the artists of the Blaue Reiter were dispersed, and the volume was never realized.

During the years 1911 to 1913 Kandinsky's style moved steadily toward a more complete abstraction. His vocabulary of images was progressively reduced to shapes and colors that stand for objects. The earliest watercolors in the Guggenheim Museum's collection were executed at this time. In *Untitled* (ca. 1911, cat. no. 1), which was included in the second Blaue Reiter exhibition, motifs typical of Kandinsky's work of the period have been identified. A boat with oars dipped into a small wave of water appears in the lower center of the composition, while two lovers recline in a garden above. Elegant yet emphatic strokes of black ink that dominate the composition delineate more delicate watercolor forms and areas of wash. The same elliptical shape of a boat with two pairs of double lines for oars seen in this work also occupies the upper right side of another untitled watercolor from about 1911–12 (cat. no. 2). Hanging precipitously from the crest of a swelling ocean wave, the boat and other images are here restricted primarily to the bounds of an oval field that is defined by a dark, India ink border. Accents of bronze-powder paint reflect the influence of Jugendstil artists, who frequently used metallic pigments in their works.

Many of the watercolors that Kandinsky executed between 1910 and 1914 are directly related to or are studies for contemporary oil paintings.[24] For example, *Study for "Improvisation 28" (Second Version)* (1911–12, cat. no. 3), a preparatory watercolor, is extremely close to the second oil version of *Improvisation 28* (Collection Solomon R. Guggenheim Museum, New York). However, certain elements, such as the mountain and cylinder of a cannon in the top left corner and the citadel and sun at the upper right, have been obscured in the final version.[25]

In other cases, such as *Study for "Improvisation 33 (Orient I)"* (1913, cat. no. 5), it is almost impossible to distinguish specific images without the aid of other studies and the final painting (Collection Stedelijk Museum, Amsterdam). Kandinsky painted two additional watercolor sketches for *Improvisation 33 (Orient I)*, both of which are in the collection of the Lenbachhaus, Munich. In these works (see fig. 9, for example) a female figure with rounded breasts reclines across the foreground, while the slender, lofty form of a minaret rises above. To the right of the tower an arching blue curve describes the shape of a fountain of water. The degree to which images in the study have been abstracted parallels that of the oil, although the torso and breasts of the woman in the painting are closer to the studies in Munich. However, the recognizable subjects here are secondary in importance to the expressive qualities of line and color, and it is significant that all four works display similar compositions and analogous pictorial elements. *Improvisation 33 (Orient I)* and its studies share the same distinctive, diagonal strokes of color in the upper left corner, the blue arch and red circle to the right, and the dabs of pigment in the middle ground and along the bottom edge. The rhythmic forms, energetic brush strokes, and translucent tones of red, yellow, and blue that animate this group also characterize much of Kandinsky's production at this phase of his career.

9. One of three watercolor sketches for
Improvisation 33 (Orient 1), 1913.
(Watercolor and India ink on paper,
9 7/16 x 11 15/16 inches.)
Städtische Galerie im Lenbachhaus, Munich
(GMS 359)

Kandinsky made as many as eighteen drawings, watercolors, and oil studies for *Bild mit weissem Rand (Painting with White Border,* fig. 10), a major canvas from 1913 that was included in Solomon Guggenheim's original gift to his foundation.[26] One of the studies (cat. no. 7) belongs to the Hilla von Rebay Foundation. Having returned to Munich in mid-December of 1912 from a two-month visit to Russia, Kandinsky began to record his impressions of Moscow in sketches for the oil, which he would not complete for five months. The studies, which range in date from December 1912 through May 1913, and a text that he wrote on the painting, help to decipher the artist's highly personal iconography. In all but the most schematic renderings, the three distinctive, curving, black lines of the motif of the troika, a Russian sled pulled by three horses, fill the upper left corner. The central image of the horse and rider has been identified as St. George because of the prominent lance that the knight wields.[27] The spear in the Rebay watercolor is painted red and cuts diagonally across almost the entire sheet of paper. In the oil, the lance is white and occupies a smaller, though no less important, position in the middle of the composition. In both versions, the head and back of the horse and rider are suggested by a black line that forms a triple-humped curve in the center. One of the sketches in the Lenbachhaus demonstrates how Kandinsky practiced drawing his emblematic interpretation of the motif (fig. 11). Wavy black lines in the oil and some of the studies stand for the horse's tail. The fish forms and other details that appear quite clearly on the right of the Rebay study and less precisely in other works are subsumed completely in the painting by the white border. Kandinsky used the border to define the right edge of the canvas, then named the painting for the device that ultimately enabled him to resolve the composition.[28]

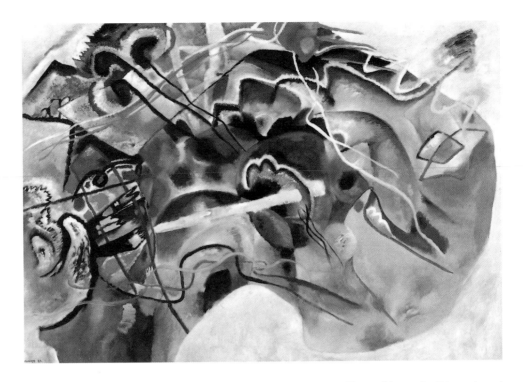

In December 1913 Kandinsky completed two oils, *Helles Bild* (*Light Picture*) and *Schwarze Linien* (*Black Lines*), now in the Guggenheim Museum collection, that the artist considered to be among his earliest non-objective paintings (see fig. 12, for example). Kandinsky adopted specific aspects of his works on paper—in particular the handling of pigment, translucent coloration, and delicate tracery of fine lines—to create his first totally abstract pictures. Thus, the advances made in the works on paper not only anticipated Kandinsky's stylistic development in other media, but also helped the artist achieve his breakthrough to non-objective painting.

Although some scholars have attempted to relate these works to earlier compositions with more explicit cosmic or landscape subjects, Kandinsky's own writings confirm the departure of his art from the world of recognizable objects. In the first editions of *On the Spiritual in Art*, published in 1911 and 1912, Kandinsky cautioned against a completely abstract art: "Today, the artist cannot manage exclusively with purely abstract forms. These forms are too imprecise for him. To limit oneself exclusively to the imprecise is to deprive oneself of possibilities, to exclude the purely human and thus impoverish one's means of expression."[29] In 1914, as his own art evolved toward ever-more-complete abstraction, Kandinsky rewrote the essential passage for subsequent editions of the book to read: "Today, *only few artists* can manage with purely abstract forms. These forms are *often* too imprecise for the artist. *It seems to him*: to limit oneself exclusively to the imprecise is to deprive oneself of possibilities, to exclude the purely human and thus impoverish one's means of expression. *At the same time, however, abstract form is, even today, already being experienced as something purely precise and employed* as the sole material in pictorial works. External 'impoverishment' is transformed into inner enrichment."[30] And later, in correspondence with Hilla Rebay, the artist confirmed Rebay's definition of the non-objective and referred to both *Light Picture* and *Black Lines* not as abstractions but as non-objective paintings.[31] By this time, Kandinsky had strengthened his conviction in the spiritual rather than material content of art, and his own work had reached the ultimate conclusion of the problem of the dematerialization of the object that he had first encountered in the paintings of Monet. No doubt Kandinsky's interest in the relationship between art and music, in the physical sciences, and in theosophy, spiritualism, and the occult, helped him to arrive at an art whose only subject is the "harmony of color and form."

12. *Black Lines* (December 1913), among the earliest examples of Kandinsky's fully non-objective painting. (Oil on canvas, 51 x 51 ⅛ inches.)
Solomon R. Guggenheim Museum
Gift, Solomon R. Guggenheim, 1937

In August 1914 the outbreak of World War I forced Kandinsky to leave Germany. Because of the war, Kandinsky was separated from Münter, his companion of more than a decade. Although they were briefly reunited in Stockholm for three months in 1915–16, Kandinsky spent the next six years in Moscow, during which time he met and married Nina von Andreevskaia. Münter did not return to Germany until 1920.

Kandinsky did not paint any oils in 1915 and executed relatively few canvases in the next six years, although he did create watercolors, drawings, prints, and glass paintings between 1915 and 1919. Certain examples, such as *Untitled* (1915, cat. no. 8), demonstrate little change from Kandinsky's style prior to the war, and images recognizable from the Munich works frequently reemerge. During a visit to Stockholm from December 1915 to March 1916 Kandinsky executed a group of fourteen watercolors that he called "bagatelles" or "trifles." Filled with Biedermeier motifs, landscapes, views of Moscow, and other whimsical images of late-nineteenth-century upper-middle-class society that the artist had depicted during his early years in Munich, the bagatelles represent a curious moment in Kandinsky's career. The joyful, rather idyllic quality of the works is conveyed through their light, pastel shades and fluid, playful use of line. One example, *Piknik* (*Picnic*, cat. no. 9), was included in Kandinsky's solo exhibition at Galerie Gummesons in Stockholm in February 1916. Some scholars have suggested that Kandinsky was aware of the salability of representational works.[32] However, in a letter to Münter dated November 16, the artist explained:

> I am working a lot in watercolor. It's very precise work and I have, so to speak, to learn the silversmith's art. They prepare me for the large paintings which are slowly taking shape in my soul. I would like to make a large painting with enormous depth and achieve an effect of great distance with subtle means which one discovers only by coming close to the canvas—an idea which I have already explored in the paintings you have seen—but now I understand it in a broader and more practical sense, which is the result of the many watercolors done recently.[33]

Kandinsky's work in Russia was, at first, tentative and retrogressive in style and many of his watercolors display the free, energetic brushwork and reliance on pure, vivid color that characterize the later Munich works (cat. nos. 8 and 14, for example). In 1917 he began to explore the pictorial possibilities of oval forms (see cat. nos. 10, 11, and 15), while the border device he had initially worked out in *Painting with White Border* recurs through works into the 1920s. Many of the artist's titles from this period include either the word "oval" or "border." In *Study for "Gray Oval"* (1917, cat. no. 10), the border surrounds the entire rectangular periphery of the page and creates a central oval field. Within this dark focal area, images of trees, hills, and a boat with a mast are rendered with energetic curving, zigzag, and hatch-like lines. Triangular shapes dominate the composition and the animated brushwork and contrasting areas of light and dark all contribute to the sense of tumultuous activity. The watercolor is a study for an oil whose whereabouts are unknown.[34]

During the course of his six years in Russia, Kandinsky became increasingly involved with administrative, editorial, and educational activities for several of the institutions and cultural programs that the Soviets established. In January 1918 he was made a member of IZO, the Department of Visual Arts within Narkompros (or NKP), the People's Commissariat for Enlightenment. That July he became the director of the theater and film sections of IZO NKP and also became editor of one of the organization's publications. Kandinsky taught at the Svomas (Free State Art Studios) in Moscow and in October was named head of a studio.

Not surprisingly, this was also a time of great stylistic diversity for the artist. In two untitled watercolors from January and March 1918 (cat. nos. 12 and 13), vaguely recognizable images of cities, mountains, and boats intermingle with freely moving amorphous forms and more regular shapes that suggest a growing interest in the points, lines, angles, and solids that his Russian colleagues had already adopted. The predominantly pastel palette of the works and the attention to delicate, linear details bring to mind the bagatelles, while the border device in the lower right quadrant of each picture again refers to earlier inventions. However, even though the borders in these examples are incomplete, they have the effect of liberating the composition from the limitations of the picture plane. Forms seem to advance and recede in space, floating in different directions as if the laws of gravity had been mysteriously and irrevocably suspended. Many of Kandinsky's colleagues, in particular Kazimir Malevich and El Lissitzky, were interested in elaborating new concepts of pictorial structure and perspective around this time and created non-objective, geometric compositions that appear to be governed by internal rather than natural forces.

In 1919 Kandinsky helped to establish the Museums of Painterly Culture in IZO NKP and, in 1920, Inkhuk, the Institute of Artistic Culture; he proposed the

13. facing page: *Small Worlds VII* (1922), from a portfolio of twelve prints with geometric shapes. (Color lithograph; image: 10 ³/₄ x 9 ¹/₄ inches.)
Solomon R. Guggenheim Museum
Hilla Rebay Collection

educational program for the latter that June. The following October he co-founded RAKhN, the Russian Academy of Artistic Sciences.

That fall Kandinsky received an invitation to visit the Bauhaus, the school of art and applied design that the architect Walter Gropius had founded in Weimar, Germany, a year and a half before. The creation of the Bauhaus coincided with the establishment of the Weimar Republic and the school shared the government's utopian aspirations for an egalitarian society. A central tenet of the Bauhaus philosophy was that a collective unity of architects, artists, and craftsmen would create a new art to serve the new society that was emerging after the war. To this end, Gropius assembled a remarkable faculty of masters of many disciplines. Kandinsky, Lyonel Feininger, Johannes Itten, Klee, Moholy-Nagy, and Oskar Schlemmer were among those who taught painting, the graphic arts, and stage design. Workshops in furniture, metalworking, and textiles were also offered. Josef Albers and Marcel Breuer, who had been Bauhaus students, joined the faculty after the school moved to Dessau in 1925.

By 1920 the artistic climate in Russia had begun to change: the government increasingly opposed progressive art and many of the new cultural organizations were dissolved. Kandinsky and Nina left their homeland for the last time and arrived in Berlin in December of 1921. Kandinsky was offered a position at the Bauhaus in March 1922 and moved to Weimar in June. Soon thereafter, Kandinsky designed wall paintings for the entrance room of a projected art museum. In the murals, which were exhibited in the *Juryfreie* show of 1922 in Berlin, the artist combined free, lyrical forms with geometric shapes—circles, squares, and lines arranged in rows and along emphatic diagonal axes.[35] Kandinsky also began work on a portfolio of twelve woodcuts, drypoints, and lithographs entitled *Kleine Welten* (*Small Worlds,* fig. 13).[36] Like the *Juryfreie* murals, the prints illustrate the artist's interest at this time in creating more simplified, schematic compositions in which circles, spears, trapeziums, checkerboards, and cross bars predominate.

At the Weimar Bauhaus, Kandinsky was named master of the Wall-Painting Workshop and he taught a course in the theory of form, which was required of all preliminary students. The theories of the correspondence between the primary colors and basic shapes, which the artist had first investigated in *On the Spiritual in Art* and again referred to in the pedagogical program he devised for Inkhuk, became the basis for his teaching at the Bauhaus.[37] The Bauhaus years were prolific; Kandinsky painted approximately three hundred oils in addition to a remarkable number of watercolors.

According to his handlists, Kandinsky executed 183 watercolors between 1922 and 1926. Most of the works in this medium are extremely close to corresponding paintings in oil; furthermore, one detailed watercolor often sufficed as a preliminary study for a painting. From 1924 until 1934 each entry was given its own title rather than that of a related oil on canvas, an indication that the artist was beginning to consider his watercolors independent of his other works and equal to them in importance.

Several watercolors from 1922 illustrate the continuing development of Kandinsky's style at the outset of this fruitful period. The irregularly shaped field in the center of *Grauer Fleck* (*Gray Spot*, cat. no. 16) brings to mind *Study for "Gray Oval"* and other earlier pictures. In *Untitled* (cat. no. 17), however, a tilted, light-gray trapezium, whose corners extend to all four edges of the paper, takes the place of the central oval shape. The painted corners of another untitled watercolor (cat. no. 18)—remnants of the border devices prevalent in Kandinsky's compositions after 1913—create an eight-sided interior zone that the artist left uncovered. Like other works of the period, color has been simplified and both natural forms and geometrically inspired motifs coexist within the central area. Although most of the images in these two examples were painted freehand, Kandinsky employed a compass to draw some of the circles. Their clearly defined profiles infuse the artist's work with an unprecedented feeling of calm and order.

By 1923, another productive year, Kandinsky had abandoned his use of the border. Instead, as in *Heiterer Klang* (*Bright Sound*, cat. no. 20), geometric shapes and lines have been dispersed across the entire surface of the bare paper support. *Composition 8* (fig. 14), one of a series of major oils executed between February and July, exemplifies the same new open structure and distribution of geometric elements. In the canvas, angular and circular shapes stand out from an unmodulated, light-yellow background that resembles the pale, off-white color of paper. *Bright Sound*, *Composition 8*, and *Bogen und Spitze* (*Arc and Point*, cat. no. 21), another watercolor from 1923, contain large, dominant circles that contrast with the sharp points and angles of other figures. The works illustrate an increasing reliance upon the compass and straight edge as precise circular and triangular forms assume greater importance as formal pictorial elements in Kandinsky's oeuvre.

Although generalized landscape references can be found, the essential content of Kandinsky's watercolors and paintings from his first year in Weimar is abstract. By the end of the year, Kandinsky had developed a highly personal vocabulary of pure geometric elements that is among the artist's significant achievements of the time. Images of half-circles, triangles, squares, grids, checkerboards, diagonal spears, and curving horns dominate the artist's work of the Bauhaus period. Kandinsky had first painted geometricized shapes that no longer resembled recognizable images as early as 1921, when he was still in Russia.

Beginning in 1923, the circle became a recurring motif in the artist's work. In a letter to his biographer, Will Grohmann, Kandinsky explained the importance of the shape:

> You mention the circle, and I agree with your definition. It is a link with
> the cosmic. But I use it above all formally. . . .Why does the circle
> fascinate me? It is
> 1. the most modest form, but asserts itself unconditionally,
> 2. a precise but inexhaustible variable,
> 3. simultaneously stable and unstable,
> 4. simultaneously loud and soft,
> 5. a single tension that carries countless tensions within it. The circle is
> the synthesis of the great oppositions. It combines the concentric and the
> excentric [sic] in a single form, and in balance. Of the three primary
> forms, it points most clearly to the fourth dimension.[38]

And, in response to a questionnaire that was written and circulated to artists by the
German psychologist Paul Plaut, Kandinsky continued to articulate his ideas:

> I love circles today in the same way that previously I loved, e.g., horses—
> perhaps even more, since I find in circles more inner possibilities, which
> is the reason why the circle has replaced the horse.[39]

In *Bright Sound* and *Composition 8* the circle functions within the overall context of an
open, abstract landscape, whereas in other works of the period the circle is clustered
with various abstract signs and figures in the center of the composition. In *Träumerisch
Regung* (*Dream Motion*, cat. no. 22), painted in March, the transparent and overlapping
shapes of three circles, three triangles, and a rectangle create complex spatial tensions
and rich, chromatic relationships.

In 1924 Kandinsky painted seventy-six watercolors in which he elaborated on aspects
of his mature abstract style. In *Helle Klarheit* (*Bright Lucidity*, cat. no. 24), executed in

May 1924, familiar shapes are clearly defined from the unpainted background and are arranged more complexly. Forms in *Auf Violett* (*On Violet*, July 1924, cat. no. 25), however, are scattered across the uneven surface of the sheet, which has been completely washed with purple pigment. Kandinsky also experimented with varied surface textures in *Grau* (*Gray*, October 1924, cat. no. 26). Here, the mottled appearance of the large central trapezium and of one circle contrasts markedly with the dark, smooth, and flat silhouettes of the other shapes.[40] The distribution of forms in *Gray* brings to mind such works from the previous year as *Bright Sound*, while the same rather dark, somber colors can be seen in *Morgengrauen* (*Daybreak*, cat. no. 27), which was completed the following month. Here, the preponderance of black and murky blue tones emphasizes the crowded—almost claustrophobic—feeling that persists in this more densely filled composition. Kandinsky used delicate veils of light-blue, rose, and yellow tones to inflect the central trapezium-shaped zone of the picture, which is emphatically offset by the surrounding dark border, a remnant from earlier works. *Haltlos* (*Unstable*, cat. no. 28), another watercolor from November, presents a greatly simplified arrangement of delicate circles and lines within a light, subtly modulated field. The irregular texture of the background and the washes of color that articulate forms contribute to the atmospheric effects of the composition.

Kandinsky created the blurred, indistinct shapes of the blue circle and lavender triangle in *Unstable* by bleeding pigments into the wet paper support. In sharp contrast are the more precisely defined shapes of *Brauner Doppelklang* (*Brown Double Sound*, cat. no. 29), which dates from the end of the year. Like *Unstable*, the palette is pale, although, as the title suggests, the colors are restricted primarily to brown and other subdued earth tones. The arrow motif, constructed by combining a triangle and square, is used repeatedly in *Brown Double Sound* as if to indicate the movements of forms in many different directions; it is a new invention in the artist's visual language. The arrow was a favorite motif of Klee, who was one of Kandinsky's closest companions at the Bauhaus and who had exploited the many possibilities of the sign particularly between 1918 and 1923 and as late as 1933.[41] The word *"Klang"* ("sound") appears frequently in Kandinsky's theoretical writings and in some of the titles of his works of art. Kandinsky used the term most often when he was referring to the much-desired phenomenon he called "inner resonance" or "spiritual vibration."[42]

Only twenty-two watercolors appear in the handlist for 1925, a rather sharp decline from the previous year's production. This, however, is not surprising, given that the artist was working on a major painting, *Gelb-Rot-Blau* (*Yellow-Red-Blue*, Collection Musée national d'art moderne, Paris) from March to May, that he moved with the Bauhaus to Dessau during the summer, and that by the middle of July he had begun to write *Punkt und Linie zu Fläche* (*Point and Line to Plane*).

In June, political pressures forced the Bauhaus to leave Weimar and the school was relocated to the industrial city of Dessau. The functionalist aesthetic of the Dessau Bauhaus was epitomized in the new building and faculty houses that Gropius designed for the school, including a double house that Vasily and Nina Kandinsky shared with Klee and his family. Kandinsky continued to teach and to work on *Point and Line to Plane*, which was completed in November and published the following year in the Bauhaus Book series. (In 1947, the Museum of Non-Objective Painting published an English edition of the book; the text was translated by Hilla Rebay.)

In the book, which represents the logical, scientific development of his earlier artistic theories, Kandinsky stressed the importance of color, geometric forms, and the positioning of pictorial elements within a given composition. Kandinsky made many drawings and illustrations for *Point and Line to Plane* and also included numerous photographs as well as reproductions from scientific publications. The text covers concepts that the artist sought to explore in his own work, including qualities of weight, gravity, and space; energy, rhythm, and movement; various types of lines, such as zigzags, curves, and angles; the dynamics of diagonals; and the three-dimensionality and varied nature that he believed the different parts of the picture plane possessed. Kandinsky used his own diagrams to illustrate his observations, writing evocative captions to accompany his diagrams (see figs. 2 and 15).

In both his artworks and this book, Kandinsky was interested in exploring the expressive properties of discord or harmony created by different combinations of shapes and colors. (Working with his students, he had discovered that it was possible to convey qualities of aggression when the triangle dominates a composition; calm could be elicited when the square dominates, while the sensation of "interiorization" occurred when the circle was ascendant.[43]) *Inneres Kochen* (*Inner Simmering*, cat. no. 30), painted in November 1925, contains multiple and overlapping views of curving horn forms, a large black diagonal lance, circles, and three distinctive zigzags at the top. The tension between sharply pointed and gently rounded forms is heightened by the vivid wash of red that dominates the center of the visual field. Almost two years later, the glowing, amorphous center of this watercolor would be recalled in *Aufsteigende Wärme* (*Rising Warmth*, September 1927, cat. no. 33).

In an example from December 1925 entitled *Zwei Zickzacks* (*Two Zigzags*, cat. no. 31), the acute angles of the irregularly shaped border mirror the distinctive profiles of the black and white zigzags for which the picture is named. Contrasts between dark and light areas enhance the rather strident mood of the work. A sense of calm and permanence pervades *Stabiles* (*Stable Forms*, cat. no. 32), another watercolor that dates from the same month. Here, the subdued palette of blues and black, the monumentality of the tower-like form in the center, and the sense that forms are firmly fixed to the ground in the lower portion of the composition effectively reinforce the feeling of stability that the title tells us is the subject of the picture.

Familiar motifs from Kandinsky's visual repertoire appear in many works of 1927, including *Capriccio* (September 1927, cat. no. 34) and *Hart, aber weich* (*Hard but Soft*, October 1927, cat. no. 35). However, he continued to expand both his technical and stylistic range in these works, enclouding his forms with nebulous halos of finely sprayed ink, a new technique for the artist. In this, he was following the example set by Klee and other Bauhaus artists, who had been spraying pigment since 1925.

In 1928 Kandinsky painted ninety-one watercolors and often practiced the technique of spraying pigment onto paper with an atomizer or blowpipe. To make *Ins Dunkel* (*Into the Dark*, May 1928, cat. no. 37), Kandinsky used stencils rather than drawn lines to distinguish figures from the ground. By changing the position of the stencils and applying repeated layers of diluted paint, Kandinsky achieved subtle gradations of color and dense, atmospheric effects. In other watercolors, including *Kleines Spiel* (*Little Game*, June 1928, cat. no. 38), *Vertikalakzent* (*Vertical Accent*, November 1928, cat. no. 39), and *Aufglühen* (*Aglow*, November 1928, cat. no. 40), precise, almost fragile, India ink lines define forms and create delicate linear patterns that appear to be suspended in the deep, ambiguous space of the sprayed background. By the end of the year, Kandinsky was combining the technique of spraying over stencils with hand-drawn lines to articulate and hold together the disparate pictorial elements of *Im schweren Rot* (*In the Heavy Red*, December 1928, cat. no. 41). That Kandinsky made a sketch for this highly complex composition indicates the degree to which he worked out some of his watercolors in advance.[44]

In the second half of the decade, Kandinsky's work gained exposure through its inclusion in numerous exhibitions in and outside Germany. In 1926, on the occasion of his sixtieth birthday, he was honored with an important show that opened in Braunschweig, then traveled to Dresden, Berlin, Dessau, and other European cities. The artist's first solo exhibition in Paris, including watercolors and gouaches, took place at the Galerie Zak in January 1929, while his oils were shown at the Galerie de France, in the same city, the following year. Kandinsky began to meet important American collectors at this time. Since his first solo exhibition in New York, organized by the Société Anonyme in the spring of 1923, Kandinsky had formed a close relationship with the organization's primary founder, Katherine Dreier. Both Dreier and her adviser, Marcel Duchamp, visited Kandinsky at the Bauhaus in early May of 1929; Kandinsky received Solomon Guggenheim for the first time that summer.

The spray technique appears with increasing frequency in later Bauhaus works. *Unerschüttert* (*Unshaken*, cat. no. 42), *Ausweichend* (*Evasive*, cat. no. 43), *Gespannt* (*Taut*, cat. no. 44), and *Wagerecht-Blau* (*Horizontal Blue*, cat. no. 46), which were executed

15. Diagram and caption from the Museum of Non-Objective Painting's English edition of *Point and Line to Plane.*

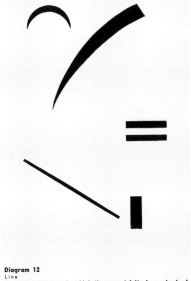

Diagram 12
Line
Eccentric structure in which the eccentricity is emphasized by the developing plane

between February and December of 1929, illustrate the broad range of effects that Kandinsky achieved by spraying watercolor onto sheets of paper. Kandinsky's expert knowledge of color theory enabled him to further explore the technique through experiments with contrasting shades or gradations within a single hue. Kandinsky was able to create secondary colors by layering or overlapping hues; simultaneously, he

16. The music room from the 1931 *German Building Exhibition*, in which Kandinsky's murals provided the backdrop for Mies van der Rohe's furniture. (Reconstruction for the exhibition *Kandinsky: Russian and Bauhaus Years, 1915–1933*, mounted at the Guggenheim Museum in 1983.)

reproduced the sensation of movement within space by varying the degree of saturation.[45] In both *Taut* and *Horizontal Blue* the entire sheet is covered with successive layers of different tones of paint and is transformed into a deep, vast field of translucent, atmospheric color. However, in *Ruhige Behauptung* (*Quiet Assertion*, December 1929, cat. no. 45), the stratification of the background into predominantly horizontal bands of blue and orange also helps to create an illusion of depth. The lighter zones of color seem to move forward, while the darker areas seem to move backward. Situated in different layers of the composition, the images of half-circles, bars, a tricolor trapezoid, and a pointed oval form appear to advance and recede in space. In *Wackelfest* (*Unshakeable*, cat. no. 47), also from December 1929, Kandinsky hand-painted the paper with a rust-brown colored gouache before painting the delicate architectural structures with thin lines of red, orange, yellow, blue, and green. Although related to the overall sprayed atmospheres in contemporary works, the dark painted ground here brings to mind the *farbige Zeichnungen* that Kandinsky had executed between 1901 and 1908 and that he would take up again in the years ahead.

Certain examples from the early 1930s, including *Hinragend* (*Reaching Upwards*, June 1931, cat. no. 50), *Heiss* (*Hot*, July 1931, cat. no. 54), and *Flecken Klänge* (*Spot Sounds*,

February 1932, cat. no. 56), stand in contrast to the artist's generally neat, methodical style of painting. In these works, Kandinsky experimented with the effects produced by mixing different media, and combined watercolor pigments with oil, gouache, India ink, opaque white, and monotype. The images here are familiar, but the rather messy surface texture and handling of paint are decidedly uncharacteristic. At the same time, Kandinsky also executed watercolors in his usual precise manner. Among these are two untitled examples (1930, cat. nos. 48 and 49), *Jetzt Auf!* (*Now Upwards!*, June 1931, cat. no. 51), *Flimmern* (*Glimmering*, July 1931, cat. no. 52), *Gespannte Linie* (*Taut Line*, July 1931, cat. no. 53), *Drei Pfeile* (*Three Arrows*, August 1931, cat. no. 55), and *Süsslich* (*Sweetish*, June 1932, cat. no. 57), which all display affinities with the work of other Bauhaus masters, especially Klee.[46] The folded screen in *Now Upwards!*, the grids and repetition of lines of color in *Glimmering*, the curved dart forms in *Three Arrows*, as well as the overall subtle, pastel coloration of this group illustrate not only Kandinsky's personal response to his colleagues' work but also his own wry, often playful interpretation of the Bauhaus predilection for structure, technology, and symmetry.

In 1931 Kandinsky again had an opportunity to work on a large scale and to create designs within an architectural context. For a project under the supervision of Mies van der Rohe, who had become director of the Bauhaus in August of 1930, Kandinsky designed ceramic murals for three walls of a music room that was to be included in the *Deutsche Bauausstellung* (*German Building Exhibition*). Intended for the playing and experiencing of music, the space contained a large grand piano and furniture by Mies representative of the International Style. Photographs of the original room and recent reconstructions illustrate how the architect's tubular steel tables and chairs complemented the environment of Kandinsky's simple yet monumental geometric shapes and abstract structures (see fig. 16).[47]

Two watercolors executed in July 1932 illustrate the continuing dichotomy of Kandinsky's geometric, abstract style. The layered, atmospheric space and shadowy forms in *Verträumt* (*Dreamy*, cat. no. 58) recall earlier compositions produced with stencils and sprayed pigment, such as *Into the Dark* and *Evasive*, while the imprecise contours of shapes and less-rigorous handling of paint in *Überbrückt* (*Bridged*, cat. no. 59) are more characteristic of the artist's Russian work. At this time, Kandinsky was interested in exploring a broad range of pictorial motifs, including architectural structures, abstract and geometric signs, and biomorphic forms.

On August 22, not long after the completion of these pictures, the National Socialist Party decreed to dissolve the Dessau Bauhaus, effective October 1. Kandinsky moved with the school to Berlin late in 1932. But by the following summer, under pressure from the Nazis, the faculty voted to close the Bauhaus for good on July 20.

The compositional simplicity and clarity of structure of Kandinsky's work of the late

Dessau period can still be found in *Links-Mitte-Rechts* (*Left-Center-Right*, cat. no. 60), which was painted in Berlin in June 1933. In *Trübe Lage* (*Gloomy Situation*, cat. no. 61), produced that July, Kandinsky introduced an amoeboid shape that corresponds to the biomorphic forms of Surrealism and prefigures the imagery of his late, Parisian style. The somber mood of the time is expressed by the dark, monochromatic palette and by the title, which Kandinsky composed in both German and French.[48]

In the summer of 1933, not long after painting these works, Kandinsky and his wife must have begun to realize that they could not remain in Germany. In her memoirs, Nina Kandinsky recalled the couple's movements during this difficult time: "Early in September [1933] we spent some time in Paris and it was at the Hôtel des Saints-Pères that we heard Hitler's speech. . . . A few days later we had lunch with Marcel Duchamp. . . . When we went back to Berlin we had the lease and our identification papers with us. . . . On January 2, 1934, our apartment was finished and ready for us to move into. Our furniture arrived in Paris that day. . . . When we moved . . . we intended to spend only a year in Paris, to begin with, and then return to Germany. . . . We thought about it for a long time, wondering whether it might not be better to go to Switzerland, Italy or America."[49] Vasily and Nina Kandinsky arrived in Paris in December and later moved into the apartment in the nearby suburb of Neuilly-sur-Seine, where they would both spend the remaining years of their lives.

Many artists from Eastern and Western Europe were attracted to Paris during the 1920s and 1930s. Joan Miró had come from Spain in 1920, the year in which Dutch painters Piet Mondrian and Theo van Doesburg also arrived. Sculptors came as well, among them Alsatian-born Jean Arp, Romanian Constantin Brancusi, and Russians Antoine Pevsner and Naum Gabo. During the 1920s Paris had been a center for Surrealist activity. However, in the next decade, artists committed to the geometric tradition began to band together and to fight the rising tides of representational and Surrealist art through associations that staged exhibitions and published periodicals. The first exhibition of the Cercle et Carré group, held in April 1930, presented work by a diverse, international selection of artists, including Kandinsky, Léger, Moholy-Nagy, Mondrian, Pevsner, Kurt Schwitters, Joseph Stella, Sophie Taeuber-Arp, Joaquín Torres-García, and Georges Vantongerloo, among others. Although the Cercle et Carré was short-lived, Vantongerloo and another French painter, Auguste Herbin, founded Abstraction-Création, a comparable group with a periodical of the same name.

By the time Kandinsky moved to Paris, he had already established a relationship with the city; his work had been presented in numerous exhibitions and he had contributed to several art periodicals. The Kandinskys filled their apartment in Neuilly with objects collected over many years. In addition to books and art supplies, the couple brought with them two paintings by Henri Rousseau, acquired at the time of the first Blaue Reiter exhibition, the furniture that Marcel Breuer had designed for their dining room in Dessau, as well as works that Kandinsky had painted in Munich, in Russia, and at the Bauhaus.[50] Despite his relative isolation in Neuilly, Kandinsky was responsive to the artistic environment of Paris and sought recognition from art dealers, collectors, and the French government. He actively participated in the selection of works and their installation in the group exhibition *Origines et développement de l'art international indépendant* (*Origins and Development of Independent International Art*) which was held at the Musée du Jeu de Paume from July through October 1937.[51] Although discussions had taken place in 1939 for an exhibition at the Jeu du Paume, the artist's wish to have a retrospective in Paris was not fulfilled during his lifetime.

17. With its irregular forms and experimental mixture of sand and oil paint, *Accompanied Contrast* (1935) represents the stylistic and technical innovation of Kandinsky's Paris period. (Oil on canvas, 38 ¼ x 63 ⅞ inches.) Solomon R. Guggenheim Museum Gift, Solomon R. Guggenheim, 1937

Kandinsky executed 144 paintings and approximately 250 watercolors and gouaches during the last eleven years of his life. His first Paris pictures contain many features of the late Bauhaus works and also illustrate his response to Surrealism and Abstraction-Création. The dominant, curved motif in *Gloomy Situation* appears in many of the oils and watercolors from the first half of 1934. The free-form elements in Kandinsky's early Parisian work closely resemble the pure, abstract forms in reliefs by Arp. Kandinsky had first met Arp in 1911 in Munich and participated in Dada activities with him in Zurich in 1916. They became quite friendly in the 1930s, a period when Kandinsky was also acquainted with many of the leading artists of the time, including César Domela, Jean Hélion, Alberto Magnelli, Miró, Mondrian, Picasso, and Taeuber-Arp.[52]

During his years in Paris, Kandinsky increasingly combined materials. In 1934 and 1935 he frequently painted canvases with both oil and watercolor and also began to mix sand with his pigments in certain paintings. *Contrast accompagné* (*Accompanied Contrast*, March 1935, fig. 17), is based on a nearly identical watercolor composition that was completed almost four years earlier.[53] In the oil, Kandinsky employed fine particles of sand to re-create the dotted, blotchy areas of color that accentuate forms in the work on paper. The slightly raised sandy patches, like the spotted zones in the watercolor, contrast with the smoother painted surfaces of the figures and ground in both versions of the composition. The incorporation of sand was a major technical innovation.[54]

At this time Kandinsky also began to favor pastel hues instead of his usual primary colors, and, more importantly, introduced into his work new biomorphic images. The artist's library contained an encyclopedia with scientific volumes, as well as clippings from contemporary scientific journals, that included diagrams of amoebas, embryos, and other primitive cellular and plant forms that have been identified in many works of the period. Kandinsky's use of organic imagery reflects not only his own study and observation of the natural sciences but also his interest in the expressive potentials of the curving, freely moving lines and biomorphic forms of Surrealism. During the mid-

1930s many artists, including Duchamp, Max Ernst, Klee, and Miró, were interested in the sciences and incorporated aspects of the various disciplines into their work.[55] Kandinsky met Miró, Ernst, and Man Ray after arriving in Paris, and their works would have been familiar to him through exhibitions and periodicals of the day. Kandinsky's own exhibition at the Galerie des "Cahiers d'Art" took place between the solo shows that Surrealists Miró and Ernst were given in the spring of 1934. Kandinsky's library also included almost complete sets of such reviews as *La Révolution Surréaliste* and *Le Surréalisme au Service de la Révolution*, suggesting that he had kept abreast of the movement while still at the Bauhaus in Dessau.[56]

As in previous phases of his career, the work Kandinsky produced in Paris demonstrates his personal response to the prevailing artistic climate. Thus, he combined the biomorphic forms favored by the Surrealists and the geometric forms employed by the Abstraction-Création group to create a new, highly individual abstract style. A prominent feature of his new pictorial vocabulary was the curved line or form, which dominates many oils and watercolors created in Paris, including *Double affirmation* (*Double Affirmation*, cat. no. 62) from December 1934. In the watercolor, the broad sinuous contour of the curve is defined by a heavy black line, also used to describe the rounded silhouette of the adjacent shape. Beginning in the Bauhaus period, Kandinsky often divided his compositions both horizontally and vertically; in Paris, he continued to explore the possibilities of bilateral formats. Here, a flat, rectangular plane of bright yellow cuts the sheet diagonally into two uncovered fields. Protoplasmic and geometric forms are, for the most part, contained within the confines of the two curvilinear images. The open structure of these central images makes it difficult to distinguish the bare space of the background from the interior areas of the figures. The same floating curve that appears in *Double Affirmation* recurs throughout Kandinsky's work of the Paris period and can be seen in *Courbe dominante* (*Dominant Curve*, fig. 18), a major oil from April 1936.

From about 1935 to the early 1940s Kandinsky often executed paintings with gouache on black-paper supports, which are considered part of his watercolor oeuvre.[57] While Klee and several of Kandinsky's colleagues in Paris, including Miró and Henri Michaux, explored dark backgrounds during the mid-to-late thirties, Kandinsky's late works with dark backgrounds are related to his earlier Jugendstil-inspired pictures of 1901 to 1908.[58] Like the *farbige Zeichnungen* from the Munich period, these paintings present vividly colored and opaque white images against an autonomous black ground. Kandinsky employed black sheets of paper in Paris rather than painting his supports by hand, as he had done during the first decade of the century. Unlike the translucent watercolor, which is little more than a colored stain on paper, the opaque gouache has a definite, appreciable film thickness and can create an actual layer of paint that

18. The Surrealist-derived curved form appears in many paintings of the period, including *Dominant Curve* of 1936. (Oil on canvas, 50 7/8 x 76 1/2 inches.) Solomon R. Guggenheim Museum

completely covers the support. Kandinsky exploited the chalky quality of the pigment to create slightly textured areas that resemble the patterns of colored dots in the *farbige Zeichnungen* and the mottled surfaces of certain Bauhaus watercolors. In *Les Appuis* (*Supports*, February 1939, cat. no. 64) Kandinsky again relied on a compass and ruler to depict the circles and clusters of beams that comprise the composition. Stylistically, both *Supports* and another gouache, *Deux accrocs* (*Two Hooks*, April 1939, cat. no. 65), refer to Kandinsky's work at the Bauhaus and his predilection for architectonic structures. Balancing the arrangement of rectangular forms in *Two Hooks* are the two delicate curving lines in the upper left and lower right corners for which the work is named. Attached to each of these is an exclamation point, one of several signs that entered Kandinsky's pictorial language in 1934.

While *Supports* and *Two Hooks* contain only rigid geometric forms, *Assez mou* (*Rather Soft*, cat. no. 63), which dates from June 1936, features both curving biomorphic shapes and the hard-edged, perspectival rendering of a staircase, a familiar image from Kandinsky's work at the Bauhaus. Two untitled gouaches on black paper (*No. 639*, cat. no. 66, and *No. 653*, cat. no. 67) were painted in 1940, when Kandinsky ceased giving his watercolors descriptive titles.[59] Although both gouaches contain circles drawn with a compass, the intricately designed curving forms that dominate the compositions were painted freehand and are derived from the natural world. Yet, a feeling of restraint and precision pervades these works and is characteristic of the group. In all, forms seem to hover in space and the brilliant reds, blues, violets, and greens effectively temper the severity of the black in these last gouaches on dark grounds.

19. An ink-on-paper study for *No. 639* (1939) predates the finished watercolor by a year. (Ink on paper, 8 1/2 x 6 3/8 inches.) Solomon R. Guggenheim Museum

In the summer of 1939 Kandinsky was denied renewal of his German passport; he became a French citizen about two months before war with Germany was declared on September 3. During the Occupation, Kandinsky's contact with artistic events in Paris and elsewhere progressively diminished. Nevertheless, he continued to work and, in addition to the gouaches on black backgrounds, he produced a group of large oils on canvas between 1939 and middle of 1942. For many of these, he made extremely detailed ink sketches, while the watercolors of this period, though not executed as preparatory studies for oils, are clearly related to paintings and are less independent than in previous years.[60]

The late Paris pictures display an extraordinary richness and variety of imagery as Kandinsky continued to elaborate upon his abstract pictorial vocabulary. The light, pastel tonality and graphic approach of *Untitled (No. 715)* (1941, cat. no. 70) illustrate the renewed lyricism that is characteristic of Kandinsky's late Parisian style. Often, as in *Untitled (No. 673)* (1940, cat. no. 68), forms become more fanciful and stylized and, at times, the elaborate patterns of lines and colors seem quite decorative (see cat. nos. 66 and 69, for example). *No. 673* displays a new vitality and clarity of means; though executed on a small scale, the elegance and grandeur of the formal elements in the watercolor exemplify Kandinsky's last large paintings on canvas.

During the war, there were increasing shortages of food, fuel, and art supplies. Unable to obtain canvas and other materials, Kandinsky painted on small panels of wood or board from the summer of 1942 until the spring of 1944. Together, the forty-eight paintings in small formats display a unity of composition, imagery, and palette. The distinctive curved form that recurs throughout the Paris work also appears in *L'Élan tempéré (Tempered Elan*, Collection Musée national d'art moderne, Paris), the last picture the artist finished before becoming ill in March. Kandinsky died in Neuilly on December 13 from a sclerosis in the cerebellum.

Kandinsky's watercolor oeuvre is as original as the work he produced as a painter of monumental statements in oil, as a master printmaker, and as a writer of poetry, prose, and philosophy. Likewise, his watercolors express the essential ideas and emotions that are found in his works in other media. Throughout his career, Kandinsky dedicated himself to an art that conveyed themes of spiritual conflict or resolution and he relied on varied abstract arrangements of line, color, space, and movement to free painting from the restraints of the natural world. The ability of music to express without representation inspired Kandinsky to seek analogies in his own work between color and sound and between line and rhythm. In so doing, he embarked upon a lifetime of creative discovery that constitutes one of the major artistic statements of the twentieth century. Kandinsky's watercolors are an intimate record of that journey.

1. Hilla Rebay, "Value of Non-Objectivity," *Third Enlarged Catalogue of the Solomon R. Guggenheim Collection of Non-Objective Paintings* (New York, 1938), p. 6.

2. Joan M. Lukach, *Hilla Rebay: In Search of The Spirit in Art* (New York, 1983), p. 44.

3. Ibid., p. 95.

4. In 1952 Hilla Rebay resigned her position, and withdrew her personal collection. The institution's name was changed to the Solomon R. Guggenheim Museum, and the exclusive preoccupation with non-objective painting was abandoned in favor of a more comprehensive concern with twentieth-century art. See Louise Averill Svendsen, "Kandinsky, Hilla Rebay and The Guggenheim Museum," in Solomon R. Guggenheim Museum, *Kandinsky Watercolors: A Selection from The Solomon R. Guggenheim Museum and The Hilla von Rebay Foundation* (New York, 1980, exh. cat.), pp. 6–7.

5. For an analysis of the artist's watercolor techniques, see Vivian Endicott Barnett, "Kandinsky Watercolors," in Solomon R. Guggenheim Museum, *Kandinsky Watercolors: A Selection from The Solomon R. Guggenheim Museum and The Hilla von Rebay Foundation*. I am grateful to Ms. Barnett, who is currently preparing the third volume of the Kandinsky catalogue raisonné, devoted to the artist's watercolors, for her original research and expertise.

6. Biographical information is based on the "Chronology," in Vivian Endicott Barnett, *Kandinsky at the Guggenheim* (New York, 1983), pp. 293–302, and Will Grohmann, *Wassily Kandinsky, Life and Work* (New York, 1958).

7. In *Kandinsky: Complete Writings on Art*, ed. Kenneth C. Lindsay and Peter Vergo, vol. 1 (Boston: G. K. Hall & Co., 1982), pp. 365, 368–69.

8. Ibid., p. 363, and vol. 2, pp. 888–89, note 21.

9. Ibid., vol. 1, p. 364.

10. Ibid., pp. 362–63.

11. Hans K. Roethel, *The Graphic Work of Kandinsky: A Loan Exhibition* (Washington, D.C., 1973, exh. cat., International Exhibitions Foundation), p. 9.

12. "Reminiscences," in *Kandinsky: Complete Writings on Art*, ed. Kenneth C. Lindsay and Peter Vergo, vol. 1, p. 374.

13. Peg Weiss, *Kandinsky in Munich: The Formative Jugendstil Years* (Princeton, 1979), p. 24.

14. For information about the twelve Phalanx exhibitions, see Peg Weiss, "Kandinsky in Munich: Encounters and Transformations," in Solomon R. Guggenheim Museum, *Kandinsky in Munich: 1896–1914* (New York, 1982, exh. cat.), pp. 40–50, and Weiss, *Kandinsky in Munich*, chapter 6.

15. For a discussion of the differences between Japanese and Western printing techniques, see Roethel, *Graphic Work of Kandinsky*, p. 10.

16. Kandinsky traveled in Tunisia from December 1904 to April 1905. Sketchbooks from this trip are reproduced in Erika Hanfstaengl, *Wassily Kandinsky: Zeichnungen und Aquarelle: Katalog der Sammlung in der Städtische Galerie im Lenbachhaus München* (Munich, 1974), pp. 141–45.

17. Kandinsky maintained, from 1910 to 1944, a Hauskatalog—or handlist—that recorded oil paintings created from 1900. The notebooks included titles, dates, media, dimensions, and information about sales and exhibitions, often accompanied by abbreviated sketches. He began cataloguing his watercolors in 1922, but did not, at first, include all of the watercolors in the handlists. See Barnett, "Kandinsky Watercolors," in Solomon R. Guggenheim Museum, *Kandinsky Watercolors*, p. 13.

18. In *Kandinsky: Complete Writings on Art*, ed. Kenneth C. Lindsay and Peter Vergo, vol. 1, p. 129.

19. Ibid., p. 154.

20. Ibid., p. 163.

21. For information on the influence of theosophy and the occult on Kandinsky, see Sixten Ringbom's writings included in the bibliography.

22. In *The Blaue Reiter Almanac*, ed. Klaus Lankheit (New York: Viking, 1974), pp. 15–16.

23. Ibid, p. 23.

24. Barnett, "Kandinsky Watercolors," in Solomon R. Guggenheim Museum, *Kandinsky Watercolors*, p. 9.

25. Barnett, *Kandinsky at the Guggenheim*, pp. 92–93.

26. Illustrations in Barnett, *Kandinsky at the Guggenheim*, pp. 102–07.

27. In Munich, Kandinsky frequently depicted scenes of St. George attacking a dragon. For Kandinsky's use of apocalyptic imagery in this work, see Rose-Carol Washton Long, *Kandinsky: The Development of an Abstract Style* (New York, 1980), pp. 126–29.

28. In *Kandinsky: Complete Writings on Art*, ed. Kenneth C. Lindsay and Peter Vergo, vol. 1, p. 391.

29. In Ibid., p. 166.

30. Ibid., vol. 2, p. 877, note 42.

31. Angelica Zander Rudenstine, *The Guggenheim Museum Collection: Paintings 1880–1945*, vol. 1 (New York, 1976), pp. 274–75.

32. Grohmann, *Wassily Kandinsky, Life and Work*, pp. 164, 166, and Clark V. Poling in Solomon R. Guggenheim Museum, *Kandinsky: Russian and Bauhaus Years, 1915–1933* (New York, 1983, exh. cat.), p. 15.

33. Quoted in Malmö konsthall, *Kandinsky and Sweden*, (Malmö, 1989, exh. cat.), pp. 31–32.

34. See Hans K. Roethel and Jean K. Benjamin, *Kandinsky: Catalogue Raisonné of the Oil-Paintings: Volume Two 1916–1944* (London, 1984), p. 592, HL 217, and Barnett, *Kandinsky at the Guggenheim*, p. 127.

35. For more information about the murals, see Poling in Solomon R. Guggenheim Museum, *Kandinsky: Russian and Bauhaus Years*, pp. 37, 40–41, and Christian Derouet and Jessica Boissel, *Kandinsky: oeuvres de Vassily Kandinsky (1866–1944)*, (Paris, Musée national d'art moderne, 1984), pp. 250–55.

36. According to Roethel, *Graphic Work of Kandinsky*, p. 13, two of the four works Kandinsky called "woodcuts" are actually color lithographs.

37. Poling in Solomon R. Guggenheim Museum, *Kandinsky: Russian and Bauhaus Years*, pp. 25–28.

38. Grohmann, *Wassily Kandinsky, Life and Work*, pp. 187–88.

39. Paul Plaut, "Die Psychologie der produktiven Persönlichkeit," in *Kandinsky: Complete Writings on Art*, ed. Kenneth C. Lindsay and Peter Vergo, vol. 2, p. 740.

40. Kandinsky added a substance such as soap or alcohol to the watercolor to achieve the varied texture. Barnett, "Kandinsky Watercolors," in Solomon R. Guggenheim Museum, *Kandinsky Watercolors*, p. 14.

41. Mark Lawrence Rosenthal, "Paul Klee and the Arrow," Ph.D. dissertation, University of Iowa, 1979.

42. Kandinsky referred to this spiritual vibration in *On the Spiritual in Art* and in *Point and Line to Plane*, which included the terms "Doppelklang" ("double sound") and "Dreiklang" ("triple sound"). He also wrote poems entitled *Klänge (Sounds)*. See Barnett, *Kandinsky at the Guggenheim*, p. 42.

43. Poling in Solomon R. Guggenheim Museum, *Kandinsky: Russian and Bauhaus Years*, p. 54.

44. The sketch, from the collection of the Musée national d'art moderne in Paris, is illustrated in Barnett, *Kandinsky at the Guggenheim*, p. 204.

45. Vivian Endicott Barnett, *Kandinsky: Vasily Kandinsky (1866–1944): A selection from The Solomon R. Guggenheim Museum and The Hilla von Rebay Foundation* (New South Wales, 1982, exh. cat.), p. 14.

46. For information on these similarities, see Poling in Solomon R. Guggenheim Museum, *Kandinsky: Russian and Bauhaus Years*, pp. 73–80.

47. The music room was reconstructed by Artcurial in Paris in 1975, and in 1983 by the Guggenheim Museum as part of the exhibition *Kandinsky: Russian and Bauhaus Years, 1915–1933*.

48. In his watercolor Handlist, Kandinsky recorded the title first in German, *Trübe Lage*, and second in French, *Trouble obscur*. On the back of the work he inscribed the secondary French title, "*Situation obscure.*"

49. In Christian Derouet, "Kandinsky in Paris: 1934–1944," in Solomon R. Guggenheim Museum, *Kandinsky in Paris: 1934–1944* (New York, 1985, exh. cat), p. 17.

50. Before Nina Kandinsky's death in 1980, she bequeathed the entire contents of the apartment to the Musée national d'art moderne, Paris.

51. Derouet, "Kandinsky in Paris: 1934–1944," in Solomon R. Guggenheim Museum, *Kandinsky in Paris*, pp. 46–47.

52. Ibid., passim.

53. The watercolor, *Fleckig (Spotted)*, is reproduced in Barnett, *Kandinsky at the Guggenheim*, p. 247.

54. Barnett, "Kandinsky Watercolors," in Solomon R. Guggenheim Museum, *Kandinsky Watercolors*, p. 16.

55. Vivian Endicott Barnett, "Kandinsky and Science: The Introduction of Biological Images in the Paris Period," in Solomon R. Guggenheim Museum, *Kandinsky in Paris*, pp. 66, 69, 70. Contains a detailed analysis of the scientific and artistic sources for Kandinsky's biomorphic imagery.

56. Derouet, "Kandinsky in Paris: 1934–1944," in Solomon R. Guggenheim Museum, *Kandinsky in Paris*, p. 51. *La Révolution surréaliste* was published from December 1924 to December 1929, and *Le Surréalisme au service de la révolution* appeared in July 1930 and May 1933.

57. Kandinsky entered the gouache paintings on dark backgrounds in his watercolor handlist.

58. Kenneth C. Lindsay, "An Examination of the Fundamental Theories of Wassily Kandinsky," Ph.D. dissertation, University of Wisconsin, 1951.

59. Kandinsky did, however, continue to assign the works numbers in his handlist. See Barnett, "Kandinsky Watercolors," in Solomon R. Guggenheim Museum, *Kandinsky Watercolors*, p. 17.

60. Ibid., p. 18.

CATALOGUE

1. *Untitled*, ca. 1911

Watercolor, India ink, and pencil on paper, 28.3 x 25.8 cm (11 ¹/₈ x 10 ³/₁₆ inches)
Signed lower left: *K.* Not dated
Solomon R. Guggenheim Museum, Hilla Rebay Collection 71.1936 R74

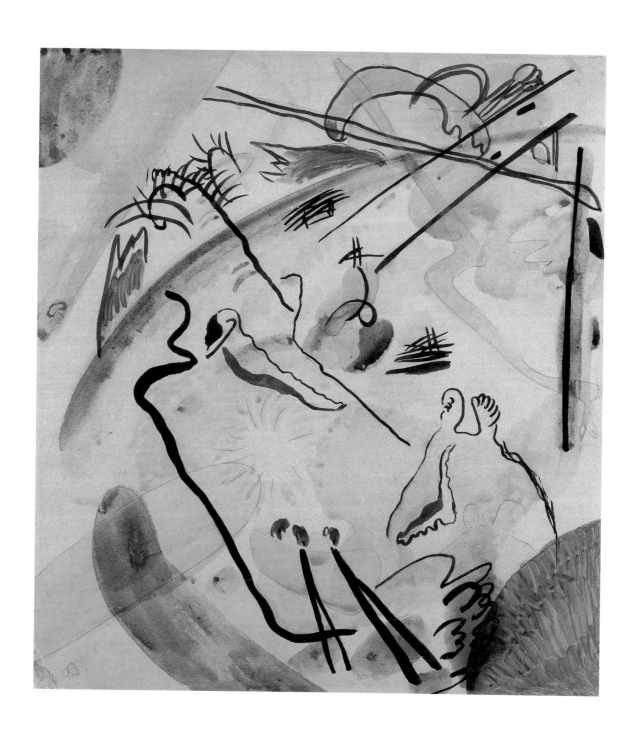

2. *Untitled*, ca. 1911–12

Watercolor, bronze-powder paint, India ink, and pencil on paper, 24 x 30.5 cm (9 $^{7}/_{16}$ x 12 inches)
Signed lower left: *K*. Not dated
Solomon R. Guggenheim Museum, Hilla Rebay Collection 71.1936 R57

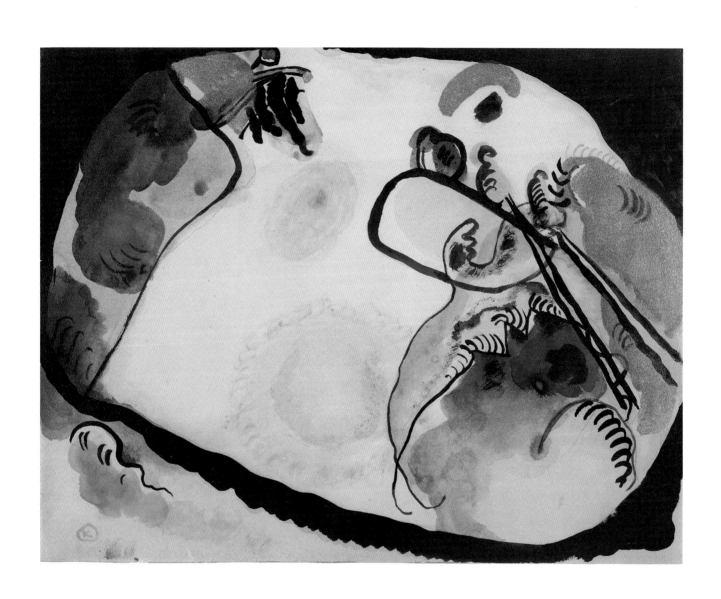

3. Study for *Improvisation 28* (Second Version), 1911–12

Watercolor, India ink, and pencil on paper, 39 x 56.1 cm (15 ³/₈ x 22 ¹/₁₆ inches)

Signed lower left: *K.* Not dated

4. Study for *Improvisation 25 (Garten der Liebe I)* (*Improvisation 25 {Garden of Love I}*), 1912

Watercolor on paper, 31.3 x 47.6 cm (12 $^5/_{16}$ x 18 $^3/_4$ inches)

Signed lower right: *K.* Not dated

Solomon R. Guggenheim Museum 48.1162

5. Study for *Improvisation 33 (Orient I)*, 1913

Watercolor, India ink, and pencil on paper, 23.9 x 31.6 cm (9 $^7/_{16}$ x 12 $^7/_{16}$ inches)
Inscribed on reverse by Hilla Rebay: *1914/Line/Carnevale*
Not signed or dated

6. Study for *Bild mit weissen Linien* (*Painting with White Lines*), 1913

Watercolor, India ink, and pencil on paper, 39.9 x 35.9 cm (15 $^{11}/_{16}$ x 14 $^{1}/_{8}$ inches)

Signed lower right: *K*. Not dated

7. Study for *Bild mit weissem Rand* (*Painting with White Border*), 1913

Watercolor, wash, India ink, and pencil on paper, 12.8 x 33.6 cm (5 $^{1}/_{16}$ x 13 $^{1}/_{4}$ inches)

Inscribed on reverse, possibly by the artist: *No I/1919*

Not signed or dated

8. *Untitled*, 1915

Watercolor, India ink, and pencil on paper, 22.6 x 34 cm (8 ⁷/₈ x 13 ¹/₈ inches)
Signed and dated lower right: *K/15*

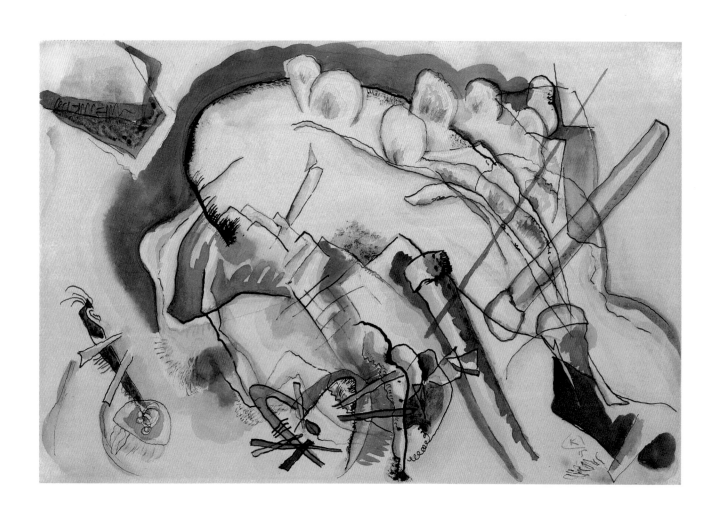

9. *Piknik* (*Picnic*), February 1916

Watercolor, India ink, and pencil on paper, 34.4 x 34.2 cm (13 $^9/_{16}$ x 13 $^7/_{16}$ inches)
Signed and dated lower left: *K/16*
Solomon R. Guggenheim Museum 47.1058

10. Study for *Graues Oval* (*Gray Oval*), 1917

Watercolor, India ink, and pencil on paper, 25.4 x 28.5 cm (10 x 11 ¼ inches)
Signed and dated lower left: *K/17*
Solomon R. Guggenheim Museum 39.246

11. *Leicht über Schwer* (*Light over Heavy*), January 1918

Watercolor, India ink, and pencil on paper, 35.6 x 24.9 cm (14 x 9 ¹³/₁₆ inches)

Signed and dated lower left: *K/I 18*; inscribed on reverse: *No 22/1918–Leicht über Schwer*"

Solomon R. Guggenheim Museum 41.248

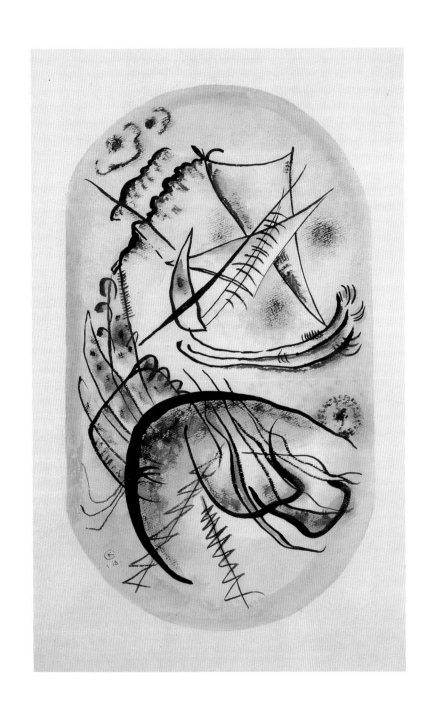

12. *Untitled*, January 1918

Watercolor, India ink, and pencil on paper, 27.4 x 38 cm (10 $^{13}/_{16}$ x 14 $^{15}/_{16}$ inches)
Signed and dated lower left: *K/I 18*; inscribed on reverse: *1918/No 13*
Solomon R. Guggenheim Museum, Gift, Solomon R. Guggenheim, 1941 41.250

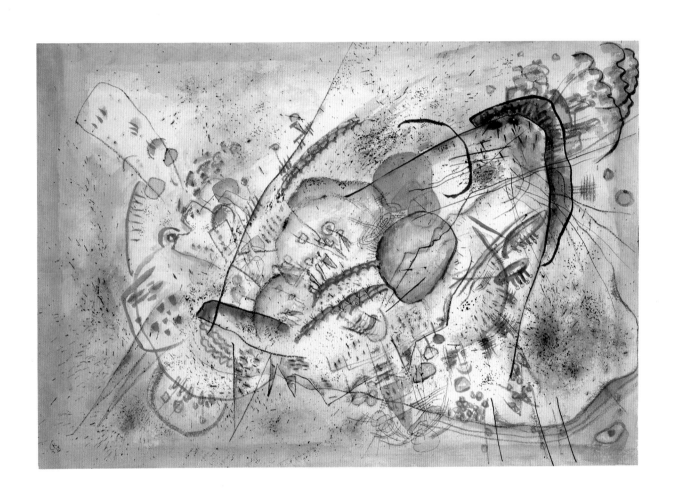

13. *Untitled*, March 1918

Watercolor, opaque white, and India ink on tracing paper mounted on cardboard, 25.7 x 34.4 cm (10 ¹/₈ x 13 ⁹/₁₆ inches)

Signed and dated lower left: *K/i8*; inscribed on reverse: *Eskiz Kompozitsii No 8. (III i9i8)* (in Cyrillic alphabet: Sketch for *Composition No. 8*)

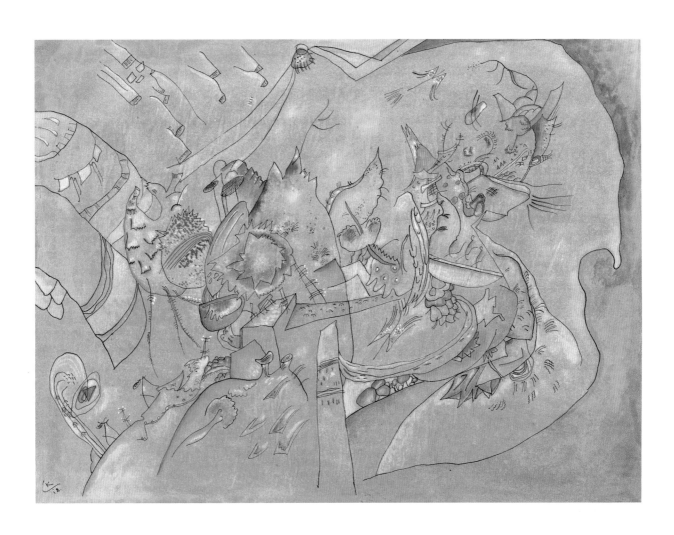

14. *Untitled*, March 1918

Watercolor, India ink, and pencil on paper, 22.4 x 48.6 cm (8 ¹³/₁₆ x 19 ⅛ inches)
Signed and dated lower left: *K/iii 18*

15. *Untitled*, 1920

Watercolor, India ink, and pencil on paper, 22.9 x 29 cm (9 x 11 $^{7}/_{16}$ inches)
Signed and dated lower left: *K/20*
Solomon R. Guggenheim Museum, Hilla Rebay Collection 71.1936 R45

16. *Grauer Fleck (Gray Spot)*, 1922

Watercolor, gouache, India ink, and pencil on paper, 46.7 x 42.5 cm (18 ³/₈ x 16 ³/₄ inches)
Signed and dated lower left: *K/22*; inscribed on reverse: *No 4i./i922.*

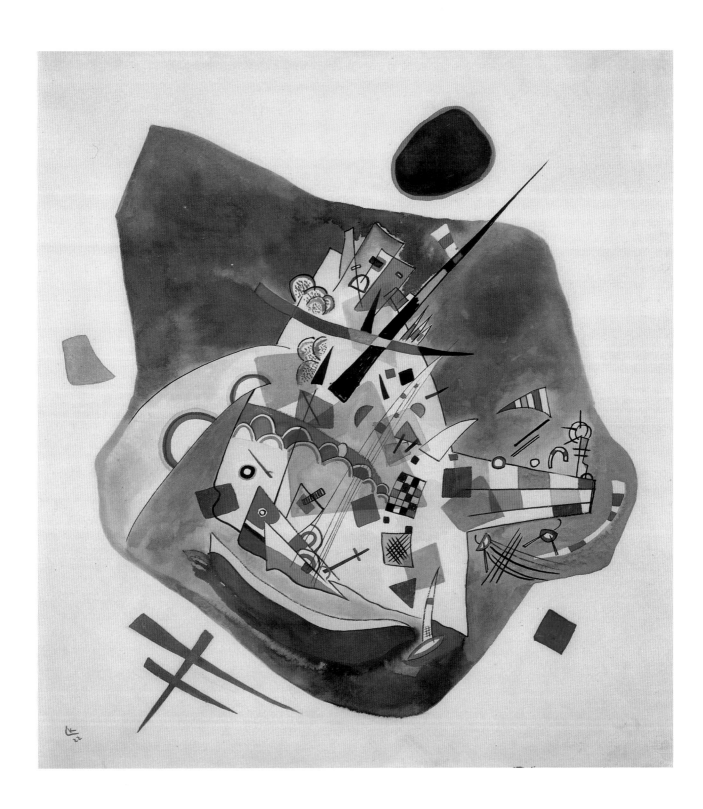

17. *Untitled*, 1922

Watercolor, wash, India ink, and pencil on paper, 26.9 x 36.6 cm (10 $^9/_{16}$ x 14 $^7/_{16}$ inches)
Signed and dated lower center left: *K/22*; inscribed on reverse, not by the artist: *No 44*
The Hilla von Rebay Foundation 1970.48

18. *Untitled*, 1922

Watercolor, India ink, and pencil on paper, 32.8 x 47.8 cm (12 $^{15}/_{16}$ x 18 $^{13}/_{16}$ inches)
Signed and dated lower left: *K/22*; inscribed on reverse: *K/No 28/1922*
Solomon R. Guggenheim Museum 50.1296

19. *Untitled*, 1922

Watercolor, gouache, India ink, and pencil on paper, 47.6 x 32.7 cm (18 3/4 x 12 7/8 inches)
Signed and dated lower left: *K/22*

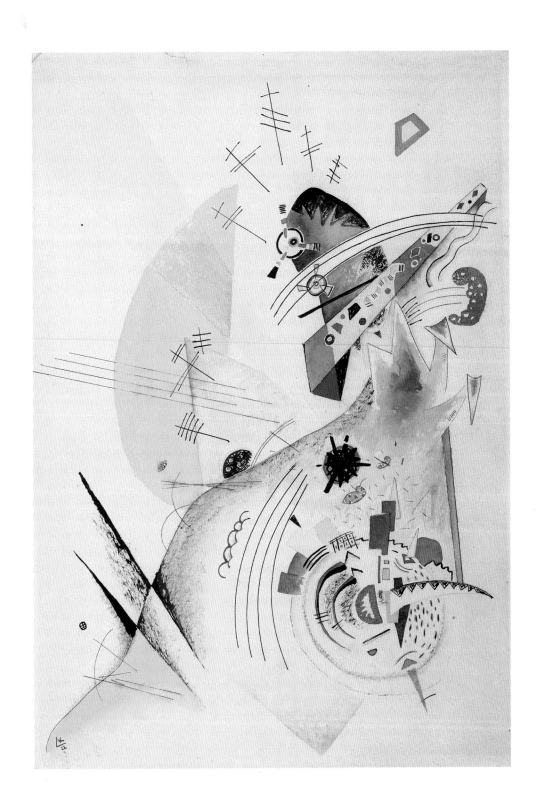

20. *Heiterer Klang (Bright Sound)*, 1923

Watercolor, wash, gouache, and India ink on paper, 36.5 x 25.5 cm (14 ³/₈ x 10 ¹/₁₆ inches)
Signed and dated lower left: *K/23*; inscribed on reverse: *No 50./1923.*
The Hilla von Rebay Foundation 1970.34

21. *Bogen und Spitze* (*Arc and Point*), February 1923
Watercolor, India ink, and pencil on paper, 46.5 x 42 cm (18 ⁵/₁₆ x 16 ⁹/₁₆ inches)
Signed and dated lower left: *K/23*; inscribed on reverse mount: *No 58./i923 "Bogen und Spitze"*
Solomon R. Guggenheim Museum 50.1290

22. *Träumerisch Regung* (*Dream Motion*), March 1923
Watercolor, India ink, and pencil on paper, 46.4 x 40 cm (18 ¼ x 15 ¾ inches)
Signed and dated lower left: *K/23*; inscribed on reverse: *No 61/1923 "Träumerische Regung."*
Solomon R. Guggenheim Museum, Gift, Solomon R. Guggenheim, 1938 38.258

23. *Freie Beziehung (Free Relationship)*, July 1923

Watercolor, India ink, and pencil on paper, 37.3 x 36.5 cm (14 ¹¹/₁₆ x 14 ⅝ inches)

Signed and dated lower left: *K/23*; inscribed on reverse: *No 87/1923–"Freie Beziehung."*

24. *Helle Klarheit* (*Bright Lucidity*), May 1924

Watercolor, wash, gouache, and India ink on paper, 50.7 x 36.5 cm (19 $^{15}/_{16}$ x 14 $^{3}/_{8}$ inches)
Signed and dated lower left: *K/24*; inscribed on reverse: *No 139./1924 "Helle Klarheit"*
The Hilla von Rebay Foundation 1970.77

25. *Auf Violett* (*On Violet*), July 1924

Watercolor, opaque white, and India ink on paper, 34.5 x 22.6 cm (13 $^9/_{16}$ x 8 $^7/_8$ inches)
Signed and dated lower left: *K/24*; inscribed on reverse: *No i49./i924–"Auf Violett."*
The Hilla von Rebay Foundation 1970.157

26. *Grau* (*Gray*), October 1924

Watercolor, India ink, and pencil on paper, 48.9 x 33.8 cm (19 ¹/₄ x 13 ⁵/₁₆ inches)
Signed and dated lower left: *K/24*; inscribed on reverse: *No 161/1924*; inscribed on reverse, not by the artist:
Vom Künstler/durch OttoRalfs/19.XII.925./Kandinsky–1924/Grau/Aquarell/No 161/925.

27. *Morgengrauen (Daybreak)*, November 1924

Watercolor and India ink on paper, 34.6 x 22.6 cm (13 ⁵/₈ x 8 ⁷/₈ inches)
Signed and dated lower left: *K/24*; inscribed on reverse: *No 165./1924. Morgengrauen*
The Hilla von Rebay Foundation 1970.158

28. *Haltlos* (*Unstable*), November 1924

Watercolor, gouache, wash, India ink, and pencil on paper, 29.2 x 25.7 cm (11 ¹/₂ x 10 ¹/₈ inches)
Signed and dated lower left: *K/24*; inscribed on reverse, probably not by the artist: *No 167/Weiss.*
The Hilla von Rebay Foundation 1970.128

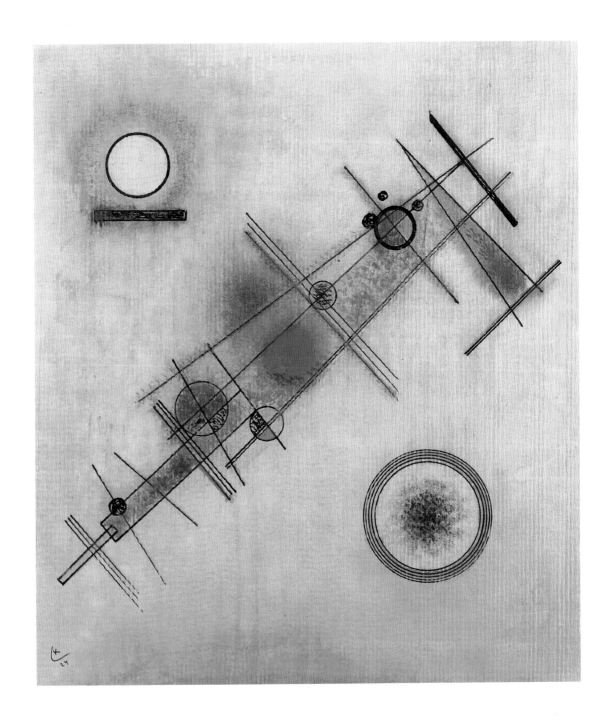

29. *Brauner Doppelklang* (*Brown Double Sound*), November–December 1924
Watercolor, wash, India ink, and pencil on paper, 48.5 x 33.3 cm (19 $^1/_8$ x 13 $^1/_8$ inches)
Signed and dated lower left: *K/24*; inscribed on reverse: *No 176/1924*
The Hilla von Rebay Foundation 1970.113

30. *Inneres Kochen* (*Inner Simmering*), November 1925

Watercolor, wash, India ink, and pencil on paper, 48.4 x 32.1 cm (19 $^1/_{16}$ x 12 $^5/_8$ inches)

Signed and dated lower left: *K/25*; inscribed on reverse: *No i94/i925–Inneres Kochen"*

The Hilla von Rebay Foundation 1970.119

31. *Zwei Zickzacks* (*Two Zigzags*), December 1925

Watercolor, gouache, and India ink on paper, 31.6 x 48.6 cm (12 $^7/_{16}$ x 19 $^1/_8$ inches)

Signed and dated lower left: *K/25*; inscribed on reverse: *No 297/1925–"Zwei Zickzacks."*

Solomon R. Guggenheim Museum 48.1172x86

32. *Stabiles (Stable Forms)*, December 1925
Watercolor, gouache, India ink, and pencil on paper, 48.5 x 32.3 cm (19 ¹/₈ x 12 ¹¹/₁₆ inches)
Signed and dated lower left: *K/25*; inscribed on reverse: *No 204/1925–"Stabiles."*
The Hilla von Rebay Foundation 1970.78

33. *Aufsteigende Wärme* (*Rising Warmth*), September 1927
Watercolor, wash, India ink, and pencil on paper, 25.3 x 36 cm (9 $^{15}/_{16}$ x 14 $^{3}/_{16}$ inches)
Signed and dated lower left: *K/27*; inscribed on reverse: *No 2i2/i927*
The Hilla von Rebay Foundation 1970.42

34. *Capriccio*, September 1927

Watercolor and India ink on paper, 34.5 x 24.6 cm (13 ⁹/₁₆ x 9 ¹¹/₁₆ inches)
Signed and dated lower left: *K/27*; inscribed on reverse: *No 2i3/i927 "Capriccio."*
Solomon R. Guggenheim Museum, Gift, Solomon R. Guggenheim, 1938 38.298

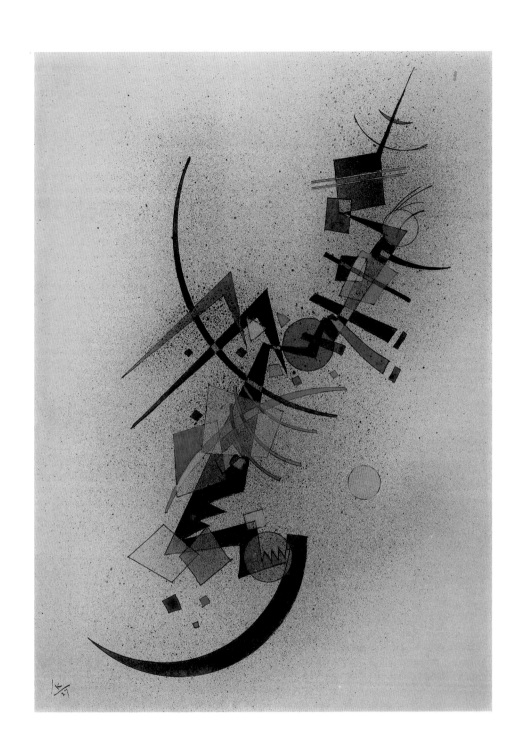

35. *Hart, aber weich* (*Hard but Soft*), October 1927

Watercolor, opaque white, and India ink on paper, 48.3 x 32.2 cm (19 x 12 $^{11}/_{16}$ inches)
Signed and dated lower left: *K/27*; inscribed on reverse: *No 220/1927 "Hart, aber weich."*
Solomon R. Guggenheim Museum, Gift, Solomon R. Guggenheim, 1938 38.291

36. *Hart im Locker* (*Hard in Slack*), October 1927
Watercolor, gouache, India ink, and pencil on paper, 48.3 x 32.3 cm (19 x 12 ¹¹/₁₆ inches)
Signed and dated lower left: *K/27*; inscribed on reverse:
No 223/1927 "Hart im Locker."
The Hilla von Rebay Foundation 1970.135

37. *Ins Dunkel* (*Into the Dark*), May 1928

Watercolor on paper, 48 x 31.8 cm (18 $^{7}/_{8}$ x 12 $^{1}/_{2}$ inches)

Signed and dated lower left: *K/28*; inscribed on reverse: *No 266/1928*

38. *Kleines Spiel* (*Little Game*), June 1928

Watercolor and India ink on paper, 34 x 17 cm (13 ¹/₈ x 6 ¹¹/₁₆ inches)
Signed and dated lower left: *K/28*; inscribed on reverse mount: *No 282./i928 "Kleines Spiel"*
Solomon R. Guggenheim Museum 48.1172x87

39. *Vertikalakzent (Vertical Accent)*, November 1928

Watercolor, wash, and India ink on paper, 34.2 x 24.6 cm (13 $^{7}/_{16}$ x 9 $^{11}/_{16}$ inches)
Signed and dated lower left: *K/28*; inscribed on reverse: *No 325*.

40. *Aufglühen (Aglow)*, November 1928

Watercolor, India ink, and pencil on paper, 45.6 x 49.1 cm (17 ¹⁵/₁₆ x 19 ⁵/₁₆ inches)
Signed and dated lower left: *K/28*; inscribed on reverse mount: *No 327/1928–"Aufglühen"*

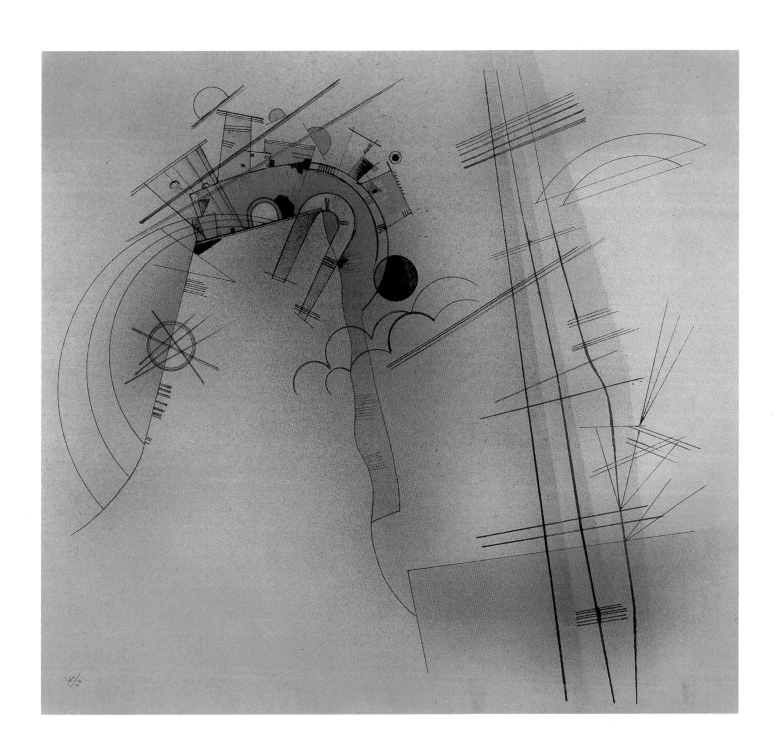

41. *Im schweren Rot* (*In the Heavy Red*), December 1928
Watercolor, India ink, and pencil on paper, 48.5 x 50.8 cm (19 1/8 x 20 inches)
Signed and dated lower left: *K/28*; inscribed on reverse, probably not by the artist: *No 333*.
The Hilla von Rebay Foundation 1970.62

42. *Unerschüttert* (*Unshaken*), February 1929

Watercolor, wash, and India ink on paper, 35.4 x 49.1 cm (13 $^{15}/_{16}$ x 19 $^{5}/_{16}$ inches)
Signed and dated lower left: *K/29*; inscribed on reverse: *No 336.*
The Hilla von Rebay Foundation 1970.94

43. *Ausweichend* (*Evasive*), April 1929

Watercolor on paper, 56.4 x 35.5 cm (22 $^{3}/_{16}$ x 14 inches)
Signed and dated lower left: *K/29*; inscribed on reverse, probably not by the artist: *No 34i*.
The Hilla von Rebay Foundation 1970.137

44. *Gespannt* (*Taut*), May 1929

Watercolor and colored inks on paper, 52.4 x 23.7 cm (20 ⁵/₈ x 9 ⁵/₁₆ inches)
Signed and dated lower left: *K/29*; inscribed on reverse: *No 353*.
The Hilla von Rebay Foundation 1970.163

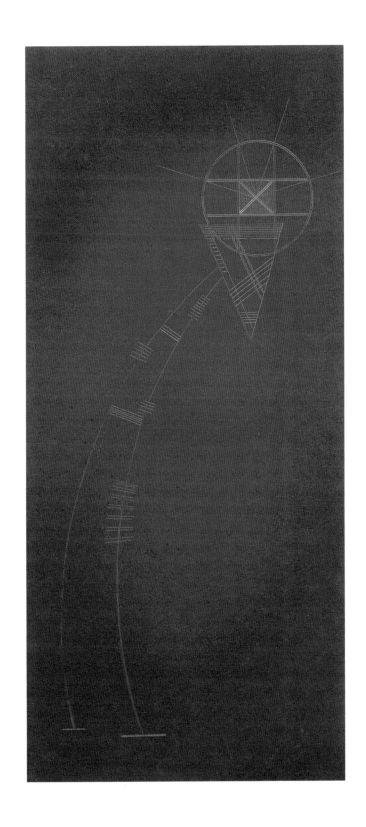

45. *Ruhige Behauptung* (*Quiet Assertion*), December 1929

Watercolor and India ink on paper, 40.5 x 53.8 cm (15 ¹⁵/₁₆ x 21 ³/₁₆ inches)

Signed and dated lower left: *K/29*; inscribed on reverse: *366*

46. *Wagerecht-Blau* (*Horizontal Blue*), December 1929

Watercolor, gouache, and blue ink on paper, 24.2 x 31.7 cm (9 ¹/₂ x 12 ¹/₂ inches)
Signed and dated lower left: *K/29*; inscribed on reverse, not by the artist: *369*.

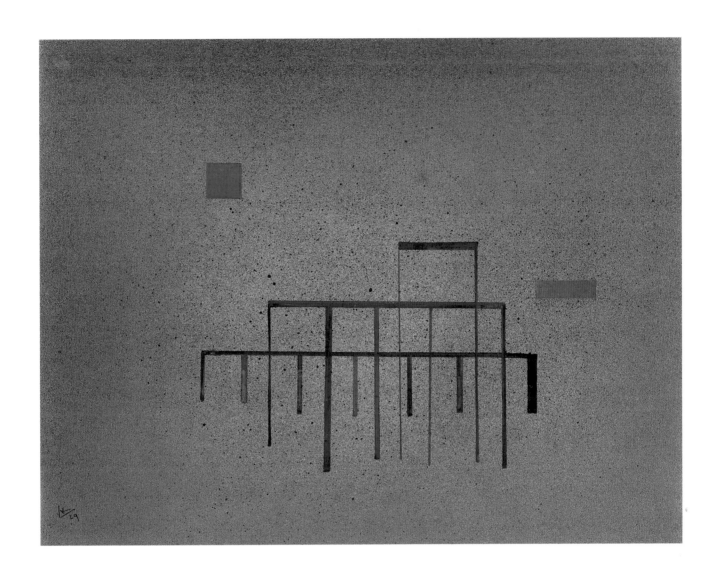

47. *Wackelfest* (*Unshakeable*), December 1929

Gouache on paper, 36.1 x 36 cm (14 $^3/_{16}$ x 14 $^3/_{16}$ inches)
Signed and dated lower left: *K/29*
The Hilla von Rebay Foundation 1970.16

48. *Untitled*, 1930

Watercolor, India ink, and pencil on paper, 21.6 x 15.9 cm (8 ¹/₂ x 6 ¹/₄ inches)
Signed and dated lower left: *K/30*; inscribed on mount lower right: *Dem sehr verehrter Herr Dr. H. Stinnes/mit besten Neujahrswunschen/Kandinsky*; inscribed on reverse, not by the artist: *"Komposition"*
Solomon R. Guggenheim Museum, Gift, Solomon R. Guggenheim, 1938 38.324

49. *Untitled*, 1930

Watercolor, brown and India inks, and pencil on paper, 22.3 x 16.1 cm (8 ³/₄ x 6 ⁵/₁₆ inches)
Signed and dated lower left: *K/30*; inscribed on reverse by Hilla Rebay: *"Staccato"/1930/Gift by Kandinsky*
Solomon R. Guggenheim Museum, Hilla Rebay Collection 71.1936 R13

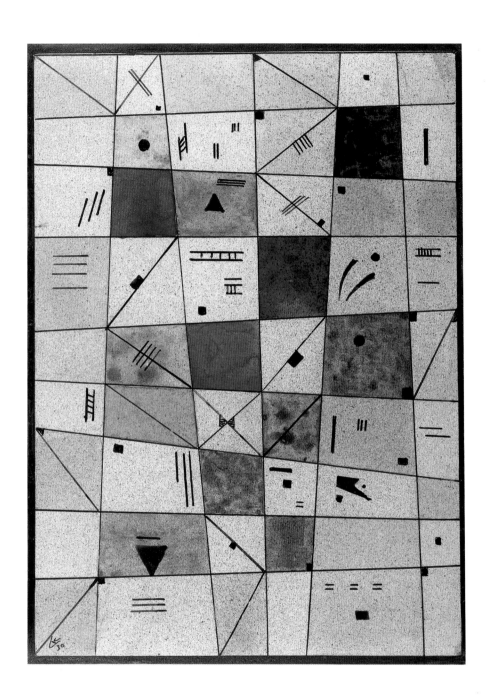

50. *Hinragend* (*Reaching Upwards*), June 1931

Oil, watercolor, wash, gouache, and India ink on paper, 46.8 x 32.5 cm (18 $^{7}/_{16}$ x 12 $^{13}/_{16}$ inches)
Signed and dated lower left: *K/31*; inscribed on reverse, not by the artist: *410*
The Hilla von Rebay Foundation 1970.57

51. *Jetzt Auf!* (*Now Upwards!*), June 1931

Watercolor, wash, and ink on paper, 48.1 x 61 cm (18 ¹⁵/₁₆ x 24 inches)
Signed and dated lower left: *K/31*; inscribed on reverse, not by the artist: *417.*
The Hilla von Rebay Foundation 1970.46

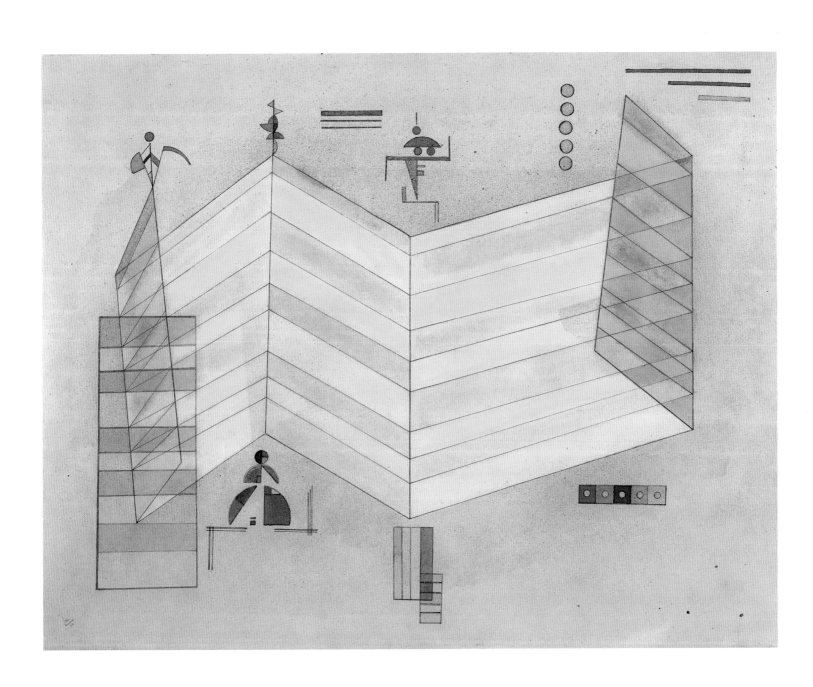

52. *Flimmern* (*Glimmering*), July 1931

Watercolor and colored inks on paper, 34.2 x 34.8 cm (13 $^{7}/_{8}$ x 13 $^{11}/_{16}$ inches)
Signed and dated lower left: *K/31*; inscribed on reverse, probably not by the artist: *435*
The Hilla von Rebay Foundation 1970.23

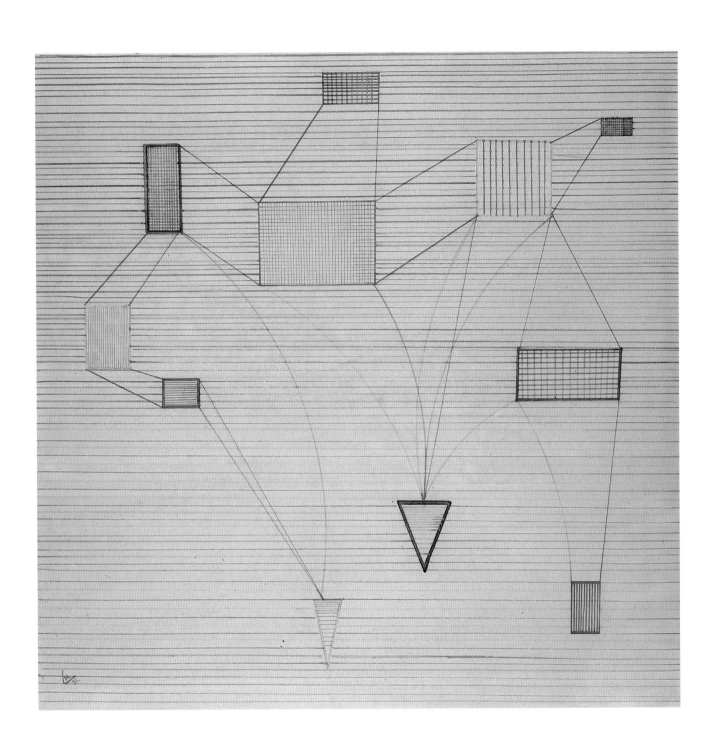

53. *Gespannte Linie* (*Taut Line*), July 1931

Watercolor and India ink on paper, 48 x 25.9 cm (18 ⁷/₈ x 10 ³/₁₆ inches)

Signed and dated lower left: *K/31*; inscribed on reverse mount: *No 437/193i–"Gespannte Linie"*.

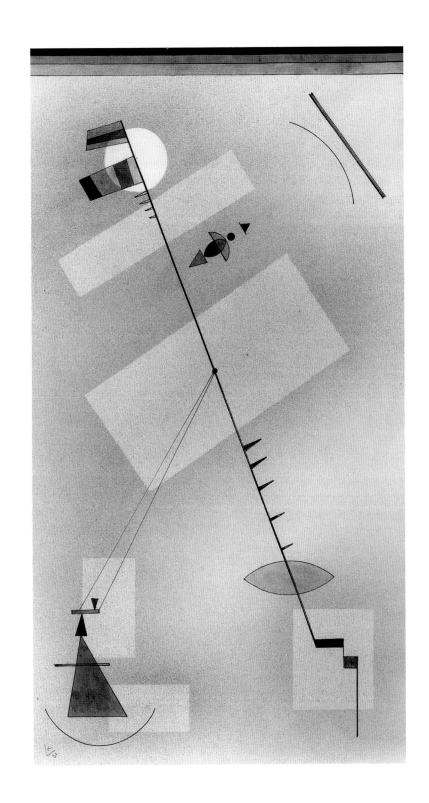

54. *Heiss* (*Hot*), July 1931

Watercolor, wash, gouache, India ink, and pencil on paper, 28.3 x 48.6 cm (11 ¹/₈ x 19 ¹/₈ inches)
Signed and dated lower left: *K/31*; inscribed on reverse, not by the artist: *429*
The Hilla von Rebay Foundation 1970.54

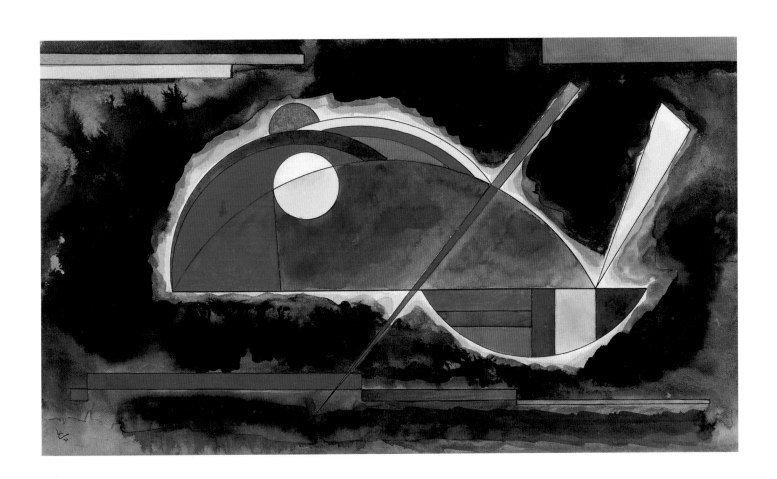

55. *Drei Pfeile* (*Three Arrows*), August 1931

Watercolor, wash, and ink on paper, 47.3 x 31.6 cm (18 ⁵/₈ x 12 ⁷/₁₆ inches)
Signed and dated lower left: *K/31*; inscribed on reverse, not by the artist: *445*
The Hilla von Rebay Foundation 1970.72

56. *Flecken Klänge* (*Spot Sounds*), February 1932
Watercolor, opaque white, and ink over monotype on paper, 33.1 x 18.6 cm (13 $^{1}/_{16}$ x 7 $^{5}/_{16}$ inches)
Signed and dated lower left: *K/32*
The Hilla von Rebay Foundation 1970.143

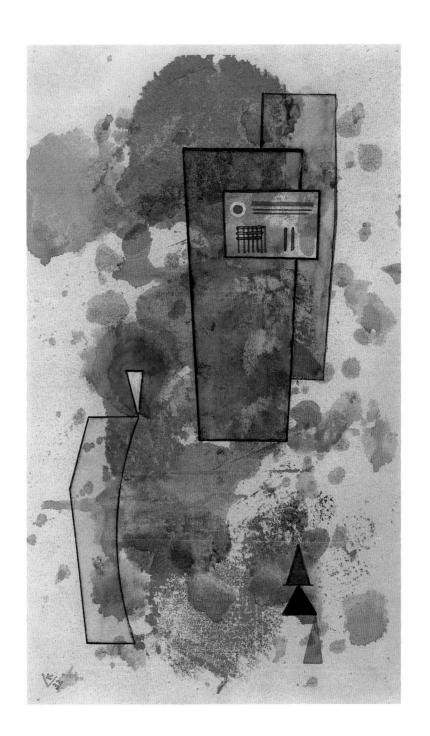

57. *Süsslich* (*Sweetish*), June 1932

Watercolor, opaque white, and wash on black paper, 50.7 x 24.5 cm (19 $^{15}/_{16}$ x 9 $^{5}/_{8}$ inches)
Signed and dated lower left: *K/32*; inscribed on reverse, not by the artist: *463*.
The Hilla von Rebay Foundation 1970.45

58. *Verträumt (Dreamy)*, July 1932

Watercolor on paper, 39.5 x 57.5 cm (15 $^9/_{16}$ x 22 $^5/_8$ inches)
Signed and dated lower left: *K/32*; inscribed on reverse, not by the artist: *480.*
The Hilla von Rebay Foundation 1970.160

59. *Überbrückt* (*Bridged*), July 1932

Watercolor on paper, 49.3 x 62.4 cm (19 $^{7}/_{16}$ x 24 $^{9}/_{16}$ inches)
Signed and dated lower left: *K/32*; incribed on reverse: *No 475/1932–"Überbrückt"*
Solomon R. Guggenheim Museum, Hilla Rebay Collection 71.1936 RL3

60. *Links-Mitte-Rechts* (*Left-Center-Right*), June 1933

Watercolor, opaque white, wash, and India ink on paper, 39.8 x 57.8 cm (15 $^{11}/_{16}$ x 22 $^3/_4$ inches)

Signed and dated lower left: *K/33*; inscribed on reverse, not by the artist: *513*.

The Hilla von Rebay Foundation 1970.161

61. *Trübe Lage* (*Gloomy Situation*), July 1933
Watercolor, gouache, and pencil on paper, 47.3 x 66.8 cm (18 ⁵/₈ x 26 ⁵/₁₆ inches)
Signed and dated lower left: *K/33*; inscribed on reverse mount: *No 517/1933–"Trübe Lage"/"Situation obscure"*
Solomon R. Guggenheim Museum, Hilla Rebay Collection 71.1936 R145

62. *Double affirmation* (*Double Affirmation*), December 1934

Watercolor, gouache, India ink, and pencil on paper, 39 x 57.3 cm (15 ³/₈ x 22 ⁹/₁₆ inches)

Signed and dated lower left: *K/34*; inscribed on reverse mount: *No 540/i934–"Double Affirmation"*

Solomon R. Guggenheim Museum, Hilla Rebay Collection 71.1936 R47

63. *Assez mou* (*Rather Soft*), June 1936

Gouache on black paper, 49.2 x 34.5 cm (19 ³/₈ x 13 ⁹/₁₆ inches)
Signed and dated lower left: *K/36*; inscribed on reverse mount: *No 568/1936–"Assez mou."*
Solomon R. Guggenheim Museum, Hilla Rebay Collection 71.1936 R143

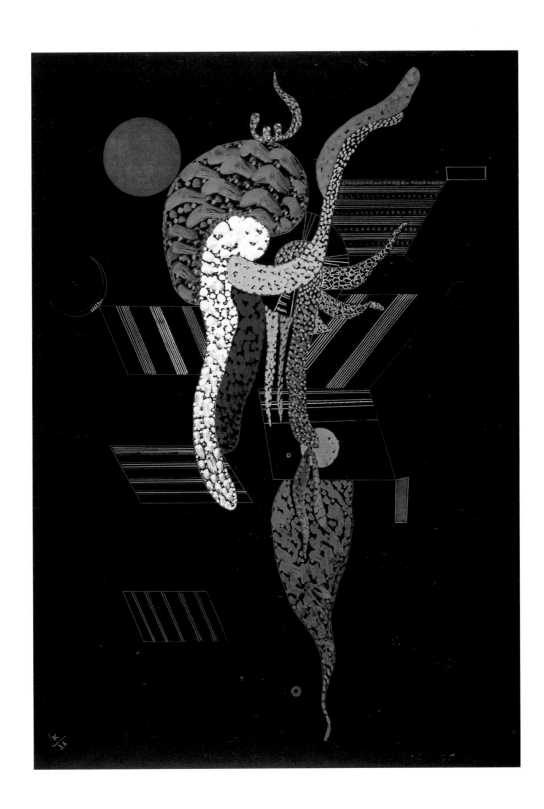

64. *Les Appuis (Supports)*, February 1939

Gouache on black paper, 49.8 x 26 cm (19 $^5/_8$ x 10 $^1/_4$ inches)

Signed and dated lower left: *K/39*; inscribed on reverse mount: *No 615/1939–"Les appuis"*

Solomon R. Guggenheim Museum 46.1033

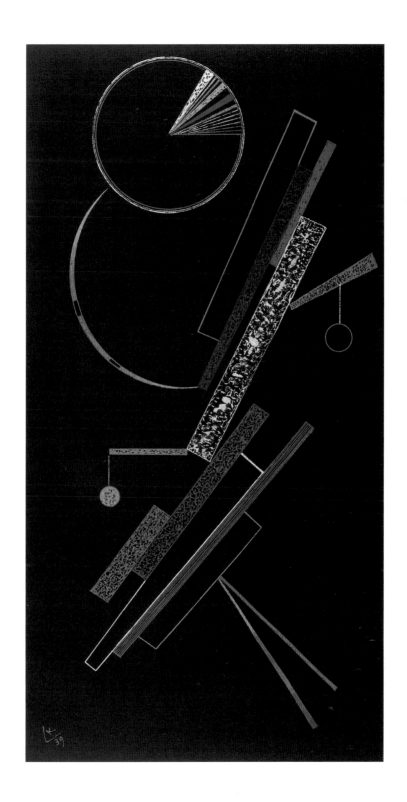

65. *Deux accrocs (Two Hooks)*, April 1939

Gouache on black paper, 49.3 x 39.1 cm (19 $^7/_{16}$ x 15 $^3/_8$ inches)
Signed and dated lower left: *K/39*; inscribed on reverse mount: *No 622/1939–"Deux accrocs"*.
Solomon R. Guggenheim Museum 48.1172x99

66. Untitled (No. 639), 1940

Gouache on black paper, 49.8 x 35 cm (19 ⅝ x 13 ¾ inches)
Signed and dated lower left: *K/40*; inscribed on reverse mount: *No 639/1940*
Solomon R. Guggenheim Museum, Hilla Rebay Collection 71.1936 R87

67. Untitled (No. 653), 1940

Gouache on black paper, 49.2 x 32 cm (19 $^{3}/_{8}$ x 12 $^{5}/_{8}$ inches)
Signed and dated lower left: *K/40*; inscribed on reverse mount: *No 653/1940/GOUACHE*
Solomon R. Guggenheim Museum, Hilla Rebay Collection 71.1936 R103

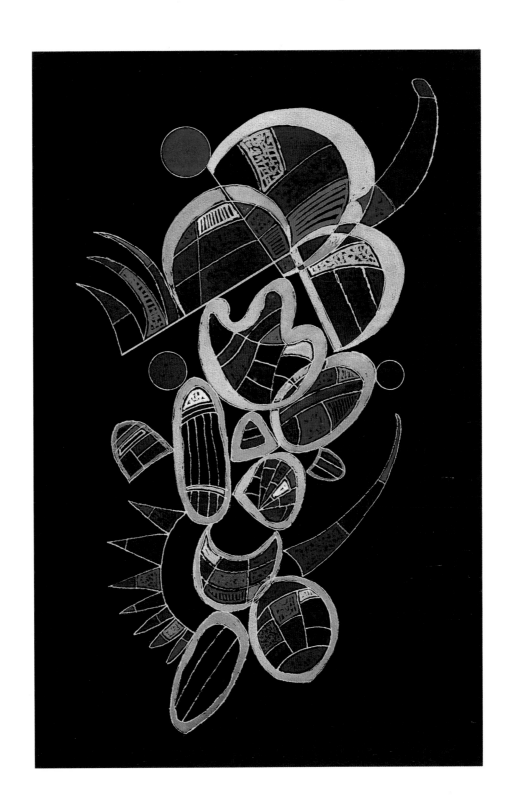

68. *Untitled (No. 673)*, 1940

Watercolor and ink on paper, 47.8 x 30.9 cm (18 ¹³/₁₆ x 12 ³/₁₆ inches)
Signed and dated lower left: *K/40*; inscribed on reverse: *No 673/i940;* inscribed on reverse by Nina Kandinsky:
A Hilla de Rebay/En souvenir de Kandinsky/le 1/VII 48 Paris.
Solomon R. Guggenheim Museum 48.1172x89

69. *Untitled*, 1940

Watercolor and India and colored inks on paper, 33.5 x 28 cm (13 ³/₁₆ x 11 inches)
Signed and dated lower left: *K/40*; inscribed on reverse, not by the artist: *No. 43/1940*
The Hilla von Rebay Foundation 1970.43

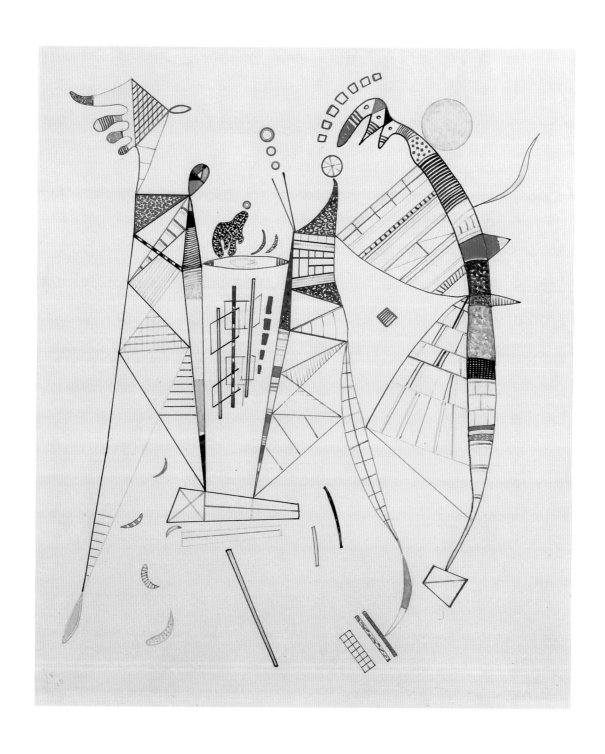

70. *Untitled (No. 715)*, 1941

Gouache on gray paper mounted on board, 47.9 x 31.5 cm (18 ⁷/₈ x 12 ³/₈ inches)
Signed and dated lower left: *K/41*; inscribed on reverse mount: *No 715/1941*
Solomon R. Guggenheim Museum, Hilla Rebay Collection 71.1936 R82

SELECT BIBLIOGRAPHY

By Kandinsky

Der Blaue Reiter Almanach. Kandinsky and Franz Marc, eds. Munich: Piper, 1912. Second edition 1914. Documentary edition in English translation by Klaus Lankheit: *The Blaue Reiter Almanac.* New York: Viking, 1974. Kandinsky's contributions include "Eugen Kahler," "On the Question of Form," "On Stage Composition," and "The Yellow Sound, A Stage Composition."

Kandinsky 1901–1913. Berlin: Der Sturm, 1913. Includes four essays by Kandinsky: "Rückblicke," "Komposition 4," "Komposition 6," and "Das Bild mit Weissem Rand." English translation of "Reminiscences" by Eugenia W. Herbert. In *Modern Artists on Art.* Robert L. Herbert, ed. Englewood Cliffs, N.J.: Prentice Hall, 1964, pp. 19–44. French translation of "Regards sur le passé." In *Wassily Kandinsky: Regards sur le passé et autres textes, 1912–1922.* Paris: Hermann, 1974, pp. 87–132.

Klänge. Munich: Piper, 1913. Thirty-eight prose poems and 56 woodcuts. English translation by Elizabeth R. Napier: *Sounds.* New Haven and London: Yale University Press, 1981.

Om Konstnären. Stockholm: Konsthandels, 1916. English translation by Ellen H. Johnson and Gösta Oldenburg: "On the Artist." In *Artforum.* Vol. 11 (March 1973), pp. 76–78.

Punkt und Linie zu Fläche: Beitrag zur Analyse der malerischen Elemente. Munich: Albert Langen, 1926. English translation by Howard Dearstyne and Hilla Rebay: *Point and Line to Plane: Contribution to the Analysis of the Pictorial Elements.* New York: Museum of Non-Objective Painting, 1947. Reprinted by Dover Publications, New York, 1979.

Tekst khudozhnika. Stupeni. Moscow, 1918. Second version of "Rückblicke." English translation by Boris Berg: "Text Artista." In *In Memory of Wassily Kandinsky.* Hilla Rebay, ed. New York: Museum of Non-Objective Painting, 1945. Exh. cat.

Über das Geistige in der Kunst. Insbesondere in der Malerei. Munich, Jan. 1912. Second edition April 1912. Third edition 1912. English translation by Michael Sadleir, Francis Golffing, Michael Harrison, and Ferdinand Ostertag: *Concerning the Spiritual in Art and Painting in Particular.* New York: Wittenborn, Shultz, 1947. Includes the artist's 1914 additions.

For Kandinsky's collected writings see:

Bill, Max, ed. *Kandinsky: Essays über Kunst und Künstler.* Stuttgart, 1955. Contains most of Kandinsky's articles published between 1912 and 1943.

Lindsay, Kenneth C. and Peter Vergo, eds. *Kandinsky: Complete Writings on Art.* Boston: G. K. Hall & Co., 1982. 2 vols.

Roethel, Hans K. and Jelena Hahl-Koch, eds. *Kandinsky: Die Gesammelten Schriften.* Bern: Benteli, vol. 1, 1980.

Sers, Philippe, ed. *Wassily Kandinsky: Ecrits complets.* Paris: Denoël-Gonthier, vol. 2, 1970; vol. 3, 1975.

On Kandinsky

Andersen, Troels. "Some Unpublished Letters by Kandinsky." In *Artes* (Copenhagen). Vol. 2 (Oct. 1966), pp. 90–110.

"Are We Ready to Memorialize Kandinsky?" In *Art Journal.* Vol. 43, no. 1 (Spring 1983). Issue devoted to Kandinsky.

Barnett, Vivian Endicott. *Handbook: The Guggenheim Museum Collection 1900–1980.* New York, 1980.

———. *Kandinsky: A Catalogue Raisonné of the Watercolors, Gouaches and Temperas, 1900–1915.* London, forthcoming.

———. *Kandinsky at the Guggenheim.* New York, 1983.

———. "Kandinsky: From Drawing and Watercolor to Oil." In *Drawing.* Vol. 3 (July–Aug. 1981), pp. 30–34.

Bauhaus-Archiv. *Kandinsky: Russische Zeit und Bauhausjahre 1915–1933.* Berlin, 1984. Exh. cat., texts by Magdalena Droste, Peter Hahn, Charles W. Haxthausen, and Clark V. Poling.

Bill, Max. "Die mathematische Denkweise in der Kunst unserer Zeit." In *Werk.* Issue 36 (March 1949), pp. 86–91.

———, ed. *Wassily Kandinsky.* Boston, 1951.

Bowlt, John E. and Rose-Carol Washton Long, eds. *The Life of Vasilii Kandinsky in Russian Art: A Study of "On the Spiritual in Art."* Newtonville, Mass., 1980.

Breton, André and Paul Eluard. "Enquête." In *Minotaure.* No. 3–4 (Dec. 12, 1933), pp. 101–16.

Brion, Marcel. *Kandinsky.* London, 1961.

Brisch, Klaus. "Wassily Kandinsky, Untersuchungen zur Entstehung der gegenstandslosen Malerei an seinem Werk von 1900–1921." Ph.D. dissertation, University of Bonn, 1955.

Cassou, Jean. *Wassily Kandinsky: Interférences, aquarelles et dessins.* Cologne, 1960.

"Centenaire de Kandinsky." In *XXe Siècle*. No. 27 (Dec. 1966). Special issue.

Derouet, Christian. "Kandinsky, 'Triumvir' de l'exposition du Jeu de Paume en 1937." In *Paris-Paris 1937–1957*. Paris, 1981, pp. 64–67. Exh. cat., Musée national d'art moderne, Centre Georges Pompidou.

——. "Vassily Kandinsky: Notes et documents sur les dernières années du peintre." In *Cahiers du Musée national d'art moderne*. No. 9 (1982), pp. 84–107.

Derouet, Christian and Jessica Boissel. *Kandinsky: oeuvres de Vassily Kandinsky (1866–1944)*. Paris, 1984. Musée national d'art moderne, Centre Georges Pompidou.

Doelman, Cornelius. *Kandinsky*. New York, 1964.

Eichner, Johannes. *Kandinsky und Gabriele Münter von Ursprüngen moderner Kunst*. Munich, 1957.

Eitner, Lorenz. "Kandinsky in Munich." In *The Burlington Magazine*. Vol. 99 (June 1957), pp. 192–97, 199.

Elderfield, John. "Geometric Abstract Painting and Paris in the Thirties, Part II." In *Artforum*. Vol. 8 (June 1970), pp. 70–75.

Ettlinger, L. D. "Kandinsky." In *L'Oeil*. No. 114 (June 1964), pp. 10–17, 50.

——. "Kandinsky's 'At Rest.'" In *Charlton Lectures on Art at King's College*. London, 1961, pp. 3–21.

Fechter, Paul. *Der Expressionismus*. Munich, 1914.

Feininger, Julia and Lyonel. "Wassily Kandinsky." In *Magazine of Art*. Vol. 38 (May 1945), pp. 174–75.

Fineberg, Jonathon David. *Kandinsky in Paris 1906–1907*. Ann Arbor, 1984.

——. "Kandinsky's Relation with *Les Tendances Nouvelles* and Its Effect on His Art Theory." In *Les Tendances Nouvelles*. Vol. 1. New York, 1980, pp. xviii–xxviii.

Fingesten, Peter. "Spirituality, Mysticism and Non-objective Art." In *Art Journal*. Vol. 21 (Fall 1961), pp. 2–6.

"Für Kandinsky." In *Der Sturm*. Vol. 3 (March 1913), pp. 277–79, 288; vol. 4 (Nov. 1913), pp. 3, 5–6.

Galerie des Beaux-Arts. *Wassily Kandinsky à Munich: Collection Städtische Galerie im Lenbachhaus*. Bordeaux, 1976. Exh. cat., texts by Rosel Gollek, Jelena Hahl-Koch, Michel Hoog, et al.

Giedion-Welcker, Carola. "Kandinskys Malerei als Ausdruck eines geistigen Universalismus." In *Werk*. Issue 37 (April 1950), pp. 119–23.

Gollek, Rosel. *Der Blaue Reiter im Lenbachhaus München*. Munich, 1982.

——. *Der Blaue Reiter im Lenbachhaus München. Katalog der Sammlung in der Städtischen Galerie*. Munich, 1974.

——. *Wassily Kandinsky: Frühe Landschaften*. Munich, 1978.

Gordon, Donald E. *Modern Art Exhibitions 1900–1916*. 2 vols. Munich, 1974.

Greenberg, Clement. "Kandinsky." In *Art and Culture*. Boston, 1961, pp. 111–14.

Grohmann, Will. "Art into Architecture: The Bauhaus Ethos." In *Apollo*. No. 76 (March 1962), pp. 37–41.

——. "Catalogue des oeuvres graphiques." In *Sélection*. No. 14 (July 1933), pp. 28–32.

——. "Le Cavalier Bleu." In *L'Oeil*. No. 9 (Sept. 1955), pp. 4–13.

——. *Wassily Kandinsky*. Paris, 1930.

——. "Wassily Kandinsky." In *Cahiers d'Art*. 4e année (1929), pp. 322–29.

——. "Wassily Kandinsky." In *Der Cicerone*. Issue 16 (Sept. 1924), pp. 887–98.

——. *Wassily Kandinsky, Life and Work*. New York, 1958.

Solomon R. Guggenheim Museum. *Kandinsky in Munich: 1896–1914*. New York, 1982. Exh. cat., texts by Peter Jelavich and Peg Weiss.

——. *Kandinsky in Paris: 1934–1944*. New York, 1985. Exh. cat., texts by Vivian Endicott Barnett and Christian Derouet. Italian edition: Palazzo Reale. *Kandinsky a Parigi 1934–1944*. Milan, 1985.

——. *Kandinsky: Russian and Bauhaus Years, 1915–1933*. New York, 1983. Exh. cat., text by Clark V. Poling. German edition: Kunsthaus Zürich. *Kandinsky in Russland und am Bauhaus 1915–1933*. Zurich, 1984.

——. *Kandinsky Watercolors: A Selection from The Solomon R. Guggenheim Museum and The Hilla von-Rebay Foundation*. New York, 1980. Exh. cat., texts by Vivian Endicott Barnett and Louise Averill Svendsen.

——. *Vasily Kandinsky Painting on Glass (Hinterglasmalerei): Anniversary Exhibition*. New York, 1966. Exh. cat., text by Hans K. Roethel.

Hahl, Jelena. "Abstraction et musique atonale: Kandinsky et Schönberg." In *L'Oeil*. No. 250 (May 1976), pp. 24–27, 64.

Hahl-Koch, Jelena. "Kandinsky, Schönberg und der 'Blaue Reiter.'" In *Vom Klang der Bilder: Die Musik in der Kunst des 20. Jahrhunderts*. Munich and Stuttgart, 1985, pp. 354–59. Exh. cat., Staatsgalerie Stuttgart.

——, ed. *Arnold Schönberg—Wassily Kandinsky: Briefe, Bilder und Dokumente einer aussergewöhnlichen Begegnung*. Vienna, 1980. English edition: *Arnold Schoenberg—Wassily Kandinsky: Letters, Pictures and Documents*. Salem, N. H., 1984.

Hanfstaengl, Erika. *Wassily Kandinsky: Zeichnungen und Aquarelle: Katalog der Sammlung in der Städtischen Galerie im Lenbachhaus München.* Munich, 1974.

Harms, Ernest. "My Association with Kandinsky." In *American Artist.* Vol. 27 (June 1963), pp. 36–41, 90–91.

Hayter, Stanley. "The Language of Kandinsky." In *Magazine of Art.* Vol. 38 (May 1945), pp. 176–79.

Heibel, Yule F. "They Danced on Volcanoes: Kandinsky's Breakthrough to Abstraction, the German Avant-Garde and the Eve of the First World War." In *Art History.* Vol. 12 (September 1989), pp. 342–61.

Hofmann, Werner. "Studien zur Kunsttheorie des 20. Jahrhunderts." In *Zeitschrift für Kunstgeschichte.* Vol. 19 (Jan. 1956), pp. 136–50.

Kandinsky, Nina. *Kandinsky und ich.* Munich, 1976. French edition: *Kandinsky et moi.* Paris, 1978.

M. Knoedler and Co., Inc. *Kandinsky: Parisian Period 1934–1944.* New York, 1969. Exh. cat., texts by Nina Kandinsky, Gaëtan Picon, and Rose-Carol Washton.

Kuhn, Herbert. "Kandinsky: I. Für." In *Das Kunstblatt.* Vol. 3 (1919), p. 178.

Kunstmuseum Bern. *Der Blaue Reiter.* Bern, 1986. Exh. cat., texts by Jessica Boissel, Matthias Haldemann, Wolfgang Kersten, et al.

Kuspit, Donald B. "Utopian Protest in Early Abstract Art." In *Art Journal.* Vol. 29 (Summer 1970), pp. 430–37.

Lacoste, Michel Conil. *Kandinsky.* Paris, 1979.

Langner, Johannes. "Gegensätze und Widersprüche—das ist unsere Harmonie." In *Kandinsky und München.* Munich, 1982, pp. 107–32. Exh. cat., Städtische Galerie im Lenbachhaus.

———. "*Impression V.* Observations sur un thème chez Kandinsky." In *Revue de l'art.* Vol. 45 (1979), pp. 53–65.

———. "*Improvisation 13.* Zur Funktion des Gegenstandes in Kandinskys Abstraktion." In *Jahrbuch der Staatlichen Kunstsammlungen in Baden-Württemberg.* Vol. 14 (1977), pp. 115–46.

Lankheit, Klaus, ed. *Wassily Kandinsky, Franz Marc, Briefwechsel.* Munich, 1983.

Lassaigne, Jacques. *Kandinsky—Bibliographical and Critical Study.* Geneva, 1964.

Lindsay, Kenneth C. "An Examination of the Fundamental Theories of Wassily Kandinsky." Ph.D. dissertation, University of Wisconsin, 1951.

———. "The Genesis and Meaning of the Cover Design for the First *Blaue Reiter* Exhibition Catalogue." In *Art Bulletin.* Vol. 35 (March 1953), pp. 47–52.

———. "Graphic Art in Kandinsky's Oeuvre." In *Prints.* New York, 1962, pp. 235–52.

———. "Wassily Kandinsky, life and work, by Will Grohmann." In *Art Bulletin.* Vol. 41 (Dec. 1959), pp. 348–50.

Malmö konsthall. *Kandinsky and Sweden.* Malmö, 1989. Exh. cat., text by Vivian Endicott Barnett.

———. *New Perspectives on Kandinsky.* Malmö, 1990. Symposium papers delivered by Natasja Avtonomova, Vivian Endicott Barnett, Christian Derouet, et al.

Marc, Franz. "Kandinsky." In *Der Sturm.* Vol. 4 (Nov. 1913), p. 130.

Musée d'art moderne, Fondation Basil et Elise Goulandris. *Wassily Kandinsky (1866–1944): Aquarelles-Dessins.* Andros, Greece, 1989. Exh. cat, texts by Vivian Endicott Barnett, Christian Derouet, and Armin Zweite.

Musée national d'art moderne, Centre Georges Pompidou. *Kandinsky: Album de l'exposition.* Paris, 1984. Exh. cat., texts by Pierre Boulez, Jacqueline Chevalier, Christian Derouet, et al.

———. *Kandinsky, trente peintures des musées soviétiques.* Paris, 1979. Exh. cat., text by Christian Derouet.

National Museum of Modern Art. *Kandinsky.* Tokyo, 1987. Exh. cat., texts by Christian Derouet and Hideho Nishida.

Orlandini, Marisa Volpi. *Kandinsky: Dall'art nouveau alla psicologia della forma.* Rome, 1968.

Overy, Paul. *Kandinsky: The Language of the Eye.* New York, 1969.

———. "The Later Painting of Wassily Kandinsky." In *Apollo.* No. 78 (Aug. 1963), pp. 117–23.

Poling, Clark V. "Kandinsky au Bauhaus." In *Change.* Vol. 26/27 (Feb. 1976), pp. 194–208.

———. *Kandinsky-Unterricht am Bauhaus.* Weingarten, 1982. English edition: *Kandinsky's Teaching at the Bauhaus: Color Theory and Analytical Drawing.* New York, 1986.

Priebe, Evelin. *Angst und Abstraktion: Die Funktion der Kunst in der Kunsttheorie Kandinskys.* Frankfurt, 1986.

Read, Herbert. "An Art of Internal Necessity." In *Quadrum.* No. 1 (May 1956), pp. 7–22.

———. *Kandinsky 1866–1944.* London, 1959.

Rebay, Hilla, ed. *In Memory of Wassily Kandinsky.* New York, 1945. Exh. cat., Museum of Non-Objective Painting.

Renaud, Lissa Tyler. *Kandinsky: Dramatist, Dramaturg, and Demiurge of the Theatre.* Ann Arbor, 1987.

Riedl, Peter Anselm. *Wassily Kandinsky in Selbstzeugnissen und Bild-dokumenten*. Reinbek bei Hamburg, 1983.

Ringbom, Sixten. "Art in 'The Epoch of the Great Spiritual': Occult Elements in the Early Theory of Abstract Painting." In *Journal of the Warburg and Courtauld Institutes*. Vol. 29 (1966), pp. 386–418.

———. "Kandinsky und das Okkulte." In *Kandinsky und München*. Munich, 1982, pp. 85–105. Exh. cat., Städtische Galerie im Lenbachhaus.

———. *The Sounding Cosmos: A Study in the Spiritualism of Kandinsky and the Genesis of Abstract Painting*. Abo, Finland, 1970.

———. "Transcending the Visible: The Generation of the Abstract Pioneers." In *The Spiritual in Art: Abstract Painting 1890–1985*. New York, 1986, pp. 131–53. Exh. cat, Los Angeles County Museum of Art.

Robbins, Daniel. "Vasily Kandinsky: Abstraction and Image." In *Art Journal*. Vol. 22, (Spring 1963), pp. 145–47.

Roethel, Hans K. *The Graphic Work of Kandinsky: A Loan Exhibition*. Washington, D.C., 1973. Exh. cat., International Exhibitions Foundation.

———. *Kandinsky*. Paris, 1977.

———. *Kandinsky: Das graphische Werk*. Cologne, 1970.

Roethel, Hans K. and Jean K. Benjamin. *Kandinsky: Catalogue Raisonné of the Oil-Paintings: Volume One 1900–1915; Volume Two 1916–1944*. London, 1982 (vol. 1); 1984 (vol. 2).

———. "A New Light on Kandinsky's First Abstract Painting." In *The Burlington Magazine*. Vol. 119 (Nov. 1977), pp. 772–73.

Roethel, Hans K. in collaboration with Jean K. Benjamin. *Kandinsky*. New York, 1979.

Roters, Eberhard. "Wassily Kandinsky und die Gestalt des Blauen Reiters." In *Jahrbuch der Berliner Museen*. Vol. 5 (1963), pp. 201–26.

Rudenstine, Angelica Zander. *The Guggenheim Museum Collection: Paintings 1880–1945*. Vol. 1. New York, 1976, pp. 204–391.

Schapiro, Meyer. "Nature of Abstract Art." In *Marxist Quarterly*. Vol. 1 (Jan.–March 1937), pp. 77–98.

Schirn Kunsthalle Frankfurt. *Wassily Kandinsky: die erste sowjetische Retrospektive: Gemälde, Zeichnungen und Graphik aus Sowjetischen und Westlichen Museen*. Frankfurt, 1989. Exh. cat., texts by N. B. Avtonomova, Vivian Endicott Barnett, John E. Bowlt, et al.

Selz, Peter. "The Aesthetic Theories of Wassily Kandinsky and their Relationship to the Origin of Non-objective Painting." In *Art Bulletin*. Vol. 39 (June 1957), pp. 127–36.

Sheppard, Richard. "Kandinsky's Early Aesthetic Theory: some Examples of Its Influence and some Implications for the Theory and Practice of Abstract Poetry." In *Journal of European Studies*. Vol. 5 (March 1975), pp. 19–40.

Sihare, Laxmi P. "Oriental Influences on Wassily Kandinsky and Piet Mondrian, 1909–1917." Ph.D. dissertation, New York University, 1967.

State Tretiakov Gallery. *Vasilii Vasile'vich Kandinskii 1866–1944: Katalog Vystavki, Zhivopic', Grafika, Prikladivoe iskusstvo*. Leningrad, 1989. Exh. cat., texts by Natasja B. Avtonomova, Vivian Endicott Barnett, S. O. Khan-Magometov, et al.

Tériade, [E.] "Kandinsky." In *Le Centaure*. 3e année (May 1929), pp. 220–23.

Thürlemann, Felix. "Kandinskys Analyse-Zeichnungen." In *Zeitschrift für Kunstgeschichte*. Vol. 48, no. 3 (1985), pp. 364–78.

———. *Kandinsky über Kandinsky: Der Künstler als Interpret eigener Werke*. Bern, 1986.

Tomas, Vincent. "Kandinsky's Theory of Painting." In *British Journal of Aesthetics*. Vol. 9 (Jan. 1969), pp. 19–38.

Tower, Beeke Sell. *Klee and Kandinsky in Munich and at the Bauhaus*. Ann Arbor, Mich., 1981.

Umanskij, Konstantin. "Russland IV: Kandinskij's Rolle im russischen Kunstleben." In *Der Ararat*. Issue 2 (May–June 1920), pp. 28–30. Special issue.

Vergo, Peter. "Music and Abstract Painting: Kandinsky, Goethe and Schoenberg." In *Towards a New Art: essays on the background to abstract art 1910–20*. London, 1980, pp. 41–63.

Volboudt, Pierre. *Die Zeichnungen Wassily Kandinskys*. Cologne, 1974.

———. "Wassily Kandinsky." In *Cahiers d'Art*. 31e–32e années (1956–57), pp. 177–215.

Wadsworth, Edward. "Inner necessity." In *Blast*. No. 1 (June 20, 1914), pp. 119–125.

Washton, Rose-Carol. "Vasily Kandinsky, 1909–13: Painting and Theory." Ph.D. dissertation, Yale University, 1968.

Washton Long, Rose-Carol. "Expressionism, Abstraction, and the Search for Utopia in Germany." In *The Spiritual in Art: Abstract Painting 1890–1985*. New York, 1986, pp. 201–17. Exh. cat., Los Angeles County Museum of Art.

———. "Kandinsky and Abstraction: The Role of the Hidden Image." In *Artforum*. Vol. 10 (June 1972), pp. 42–49.

———. "Kandinsky's Abstract Style: The Veiling of Apocalyptic Folk Imagery." In *Art Journal*. Vol. 34 (Spring 1975), pp. 217–28.

———. *Kandinsky: The Development of an Abstract Style*. New York, 1980.

———. "Occultism, Anarchism and Abstraction: Kandinsky's Art of the Future." In *Art Journal*. Vol. 46, no. 1 (Spring 1987), pp. 38–45.

Watts, Harriett. "Arp, Kandinsky, and the Legacy of Jakob Böhme." In *The Spiritual in Art: Abstract Painting 1890–1985*. New York, 1986, pp. 239–55. Exh. cat., Los Angeles County Museum of Art.

Weiss, Peg. "Kandinsky and the Symbolist Heritage." In *Art Journal*. Vol. 45, no. 2 (Summer 1985), pp. 137–45.

———. *Kandinsky in Munich: The Formative Jugendstil Years*. Princeton, 1979.

Welsh, Robert. "Abstraction and the Bauhaus." In *Artforum*. Vol. 8 (March 1970), pp. 46–51.

Werenskiold, Marit. "Kandinsky's Moscow." In *Art in America*. Vol. 77 (March 1989), pp. 96–111.

Whitford, Frank. *Kandinsky*. London, 1967.

Wingler, Hans M. *The Bauhaus*. Cambridge, Mass., 1969.

Wolfradt, Willi. "Kandinsky: II. Wider (Die Kunst und das Absolut)." In *Das Kunstblatt*. Vol. 3 (1919), pp. 180–83.

Zehder, Hugo. *Wassily Kandinsky: Unter autorisierter Benutzung der russischen Selbstbiographie*. Dresden, 1920.

Zervos, Christian. "Notes sur Kandinsky." In *Cahiers d'Art*. 9e année (1934), pp. 149–57.

———. "Wassily Kandinsky 1866–1944." In *Cahiers d'Art*. 20e–21e années (1945–46), pp. 114–27.

Zweite, Armin. "Kandinsky zwischen Tradition und Innovation." In *Kandinsky und München*. Munich, 1982, pp. 134–77. Exh. cat., Städtische Galerie im Lenbachhaus.

Kandinsky in Dessau, 1932
Musée national d'art moderne, Centre Georges Pompidou, Paris

ACKNOWLEDGMENTS

The publication of *Watercolors by Kandinsky* coincided with an exhibition held at the Banco Bilbao Vizcaya in Madrid from April 9 through June 1, 1991. The exhibition was sponsored by the BBV, which also assumed many of the costs associated with the production of both the Spanish-language exhibition catalogue and this book. For that support we are most grateful. Special mention must be made to Carmen Giménez, Guggenheim Curator of Twentieth-Century Art, who organized the exhibition in Madrid, and to Susan B. Hirschfeld, Associate Curator for Education, who undertook the organization of the show from New York. Together, they selected the works that were included in the show and that, therefore, are included here. Martina Rosa Schneider, in Madrid, provided invaluable assistance for both projects. Thanks must also go to the Guggenheim's new Publications Department, which, in collaboration with the Photography, Curatorial, and Technical Services departments, brought this book to completion.

—T.K.

My essay could not have been written without the knowledge and expertise of the many scholars of Kandinsky's works who have generated a rich and diverse body of literature and who have contributed enormously to our understanding of the artist and his oeuvre. Their names will be found not only in the bibliography, but also in the notes to the text. In addition, I am grateful to Anthony Calnek, Managing Editor, Laura Morris, Editorial Assistant, David Heald, Photographer, and Christina Yang, Curatorial Assistant, for their efforts on behalf of this publication. I would also like to express my appreciation to Guggenheim Museum staff members Paul Schwartzbaum, Ani Rivera, Sonja Bay, and Ward Jackson for their advice and assistance.

—S.B.H.